EATING AND DRINKING ON THE OPEN ROAD

W9-AHU-379

"...an opinionated little compendium.
~ New York Times

"...irresistible little guide."
~ Chicago Tribune

"an elegant, small guide..."
~ Minneapolis Star Tribune

""...a terrific primer for first-time visitors."
~ Houston Chronicle

""...opening up the world of good eating with their innovative paperback series."
~ Salt Lake Tribune

"...travelers who know their cervelle *(brains) from* cervelle de canut *(herbed cheese spread)."*
~ USA Today

OPEN ROAD TRAVEL GUIDES

Whether you're going abroad or planning a trip to the United States, take Open Road along on your journey. Our books have been praised by **Travel & Leisure**, **The New York Times**, **USA Today**, **The Los Angeles Times**, **Newsday**, **Booklist**, **US News & World Report**, **Endless Vacation**, **American Bookseller**, **Coast to Coast** and many other magazines and newspapers!

Don't just see the world - experience it with Open Road!

ABOUT THE AUTHORS

Michael Dillon is a graphic designer. Andy Herbach is a lawyer. Both authors reside in Milwaukee, Wisconsin. They are the authors of *Eating and Drinking in Paris*, *Eating and Drinking in Italy*, *Eating and Drinking in Spain* and *Eating and Drinking in Latin America*.

ACKNOWLEDGMENTS

Thanks to Doug Morris, the author of Open Road Publishing's Italy Guide. Thanks also to Jonathan Stein, our Open Road publisher.

Marian Olson (our Miss Know-It-All English editor) and Angelina Bellotti Scharlau (our Italian editor) were of great help in the original edition of this book and in this edition.

Special thanks to those who have helped us find the restaurants in this guide, especially Mark Berry and Dan Schmidt who suffered through many meals and countless bottles of wine on our behalf.

THINGS CHANGE!

Phone numbers, prices, addresses, quality of food, etc., all change. If you come across any new information, we'd appreciate hearing from you. No item is too small! Drop us an e-mail note at:

www.eatndrink.com

EATING AND DRINKING IN

Italy

Andy Herbach and Michael Dillon

OPEN ROAD PUBLISHING

OPEN ROAD PUBLISHING

We offer travel guides to American and foreign locales.
Our books tell it like it is, often with an opinionated edge, and
our experienced authors always give you all the information
you need to have the trip of a lifetime. Write for your free catalog of all our titles.

Catalog Department, Open Road Publishing
P.O. Box 284, Cold Spring Harbor, NY 11724

E-mail: Jopenroad@aol.com

Fourth Edition

Cover art and illustrations: Michael Dillon
Back cover photo: Elizabeth Enslen Dillon
Inside photos: ShutterStock
Rome photo: courtesy of APT-Rome
Venice photos: Karl Raaum

Library of Congress Control No. 2005938399
ISBN 1593600712

Table of Contents

Introduction

Can you imagine a foreign traveler who speaks basic English understanding what prime rib is? Or a porterhouse? Veggie platter, anyone? Buffalo wings? Sloppy joes?

Even people who speak passable Italian can have trouble reading a menu. You may know *ricotta* cheese, but not *malfatti di ricotta* which means "badly made," a reference to the handmade dumpling with *ricotta* cheese filling. You may be surprised to find *puttanesca* (which means *in the style of a prostitute*) on the menu. It's a sauce of tomatoes, capers, black olives and garlic.

Understanding the customs and food of a country helps travelers understand the people who live in the country.

If you love to travel as we do, you know the importance of a good guide. The same is true of dining. A good guide can make all the difference between a memorable evening and a dizzyingly bad one. This guide will help you find your way around a menu written in Italian. It gives you the freedom to enter places you might never have before and order a dinner without shouting, pointing and hand waving. Instead of fumbling with a bulky, conspicuous tourist guide (most of which usually include a very incomplete listing of foods) in a restaurant, this book is a pocket-sized alphabetical listing of food and drink commonly found on menus in Italy.

Although, now that we think about it, a dinner without shouting and hand waving is not truly Italian.

6

Of course, traveling to a foreign country means something different to everyone. For every vacation there are different expectations, different needs, and every traveler has his or her own idea of what will make that vacation memorable. For us, the making of a memorable vacation begins and ends with food.

We spent the morning staring at the Sistine Chapel and the Vatican Museum, but what stands out in our minds is the wonderful lunch in the *trattoria* afterward. Although the waiter was less than helpful (in fact, not helpful at all), the creamy shrimp pasta dish was as heavenly as Michelangelo's masterpiece. We spent a morning driving to see the Leaning Tower of Pisa, but the grilled lamb in Lerici made the day.

We know the panic of opening a menu without recognizing one word on it and the disappointment of being served something other than what you thought you'd ordered. On our first trip to Europe, we were served a plate of cold brains; we thought we had ordered chicken. This guide was created for the traveler who wants to enjoy, appreciate and experience authentic cuisine *and* know what he or she is eating.

The next time you find yourself seated in a red-tiled courtyard with the scent of simmering garlic in the night air and an incomprehensible menu in your hands, simply pull this guide from your pocket and get ready to enjoy the delicious cuisine of Italy.

In Italy and Ticino (the Italian-speaking region of Switzerland), the menu is almost always posted outside of the restaurant or in a window. This makes choosing a restaurant easy and fun as you "window shop" for your next meal.

Remember that the dish that you ordered may not be exactly as described in this guide. Every chef is (and should be) innovative. What we have listed for you in this guide is the most common version of a dish.

If a menu has an English translation it does not mean that the translation is correct.

In Italy, it's customary to order a first course (pasta, rice or soup), a second course (meat, poultry or fish) and a side dish (salad, potato or vegetable). Rarely does an Italian order only a first course (such as ordering only pasta), but that doesn't mean you can't.

Tipping

A 10% to 15% service charge is almost always added to your bill (*il conto*) in Italy. Depending on the service, it's customary to leave an additional 5% to 10%. The menu will usually note that service is included (*servizio incluso* or *servizio compreso*). A service charge, by law, is included in all restaurant bills in Ticino.

You will often find *coperto* or cover charge on your menu (a small charge just for placing your butt at the table).

Mealtimes

In northern Italy, lunch is served from noon to around 2 p.m., and dinner from 7 p.m. to 10 p.m. In the south, lunch is served from 1 p.m. and dinner from 8 p.m. No "early bird special" in Italy. Ticino's hours are the same as in northern Italy.

Europeans joke that you can tell a U.S. tourist from his fanny pack, clothes and ubiquitous bottle of mineral water. Tap water is safe in Italy and Switzerland. Occasionally, you will find *non potabile* signs in rest rooms (especially in the rest stops of highways). This means that the water is not safe for drinking.

Waiters and waitresses will often bring *acqua minerale* (mineral water) to your table. You will be charged for it, so if you do not want mineral water ask for *acqua semplice* or *acqua di rubinetto* (tap water).

"Acqua di Rubinetto" is safe to drink but can taste weird. We usually order bottled water with meals.

 RESTAURANTS IN THIS GUIDE

Each of our recommended restaurants offers something different. Some have great food and little ambiance. Others have great ambiance and adequate food. Still others have both. Our goal is to find restaurants that are moderately priced and enjoyable. All restaurants have been tried and tested. Not enough can be said for a friendly welcome and great service. No matter how fabulous the meal, the experience will always be better when the staff treats you as if they actually want you there rather than simply tolerating your presence.

Times can change and restaurants can close, so do a walk-by earlier in the day or the day before, if possible. Our full list of restaurants starting on page 100 includes many of the eating establishments listed below.

Types of Eating Establishments

Bacaro: Venetian wine bar serving snacks like Spanish *tapas*.
Bar: Bars serve espresso, cappuccino, rolls, small sandwiches,

alcoholic beverages and soft drinks.

Bottiglieria: Simple drinking establishments with limited menus but plenty of bottles of wine. Originally, these "bottle shops" served only liquor. Also called *fiaschetteria*, *cantina* or *trani*.

Enoteca: Wine bar.

Gelateria: Shop serving *gelato* (ice cream).

Grotta: Ticino has many *grotte*. These are village restaurants that take their name from caves used to store food and wine. Originally, a *grotta* was a simple eating establishment, but today many are quite expensive with extensive menus.

Locanda: Found in the country, serves regional meats and seafood.

Osteria: A tavern or wine shop. This name has also come to refer to a restaurant. These can also be called *cucina* or *hostaria*.

Paninoteca: Usually serves only sandwiches.

Pasticceria: Pastry shop.

Pizza Rustica: Common in central Italy; serves large rectangular pizzas with thicker crusts and more toppings than usually found in a *pizzeria*. You can order as much as you want, and pay by weight.

Pizzeria: We think you can figure this one out.

Ristorante: A restaurant.

Rosticceria: A deli, sometimes with a few tables, where you can order grilled meats (especially chicken).

Tavola Calda: Small restaurant with take-out or fast foods and usually with a few tables.

Trattoria: Less expensive family-run restaurant, usually not too fancy.

Tips for Budget Dining in Italy

There is no need to spend a lot of money in Italy to eat good food. There are all kinds of fabulous foods to be had inexpensively all over Italy.

Eat at a neighborhood restaurant or *trattoria*. You'll always know the price of a meal before entering, as almost all restaurants in Italy post the menu and prices in the window. Never order anything whose price is not known in advance. For instance, if you see *etto* on a menu in Venice this means that you're paying by weight (an *etto* is 100 grams), which can be extremely expensive.

Delis and food stores can provide cheap and wonderful meals. Buy cheese, bread, wine and other snacks and have a picnic. Remember to pack a corkscrew and eating utensils when you leave home.

Lunch, even at the most expensive restaurants listed in this guide, always has a lower price. So, have lunch as your main meal.

Restaurants that have menus written in English (especially those near tourist attractions) are almost always more expensive than neighborhood restaurants.

Street vendors generally sell inexpensive and good food. For the cost of a cup of coffee or a drink, you can linger at a café and watch the world pass you by for as long as you want. It's one of Italy's greatest bargains.

And don't eat at McDonald's, for God's sake.

OUR MISSION

As silly as it might sound, we have one:

No Menus in English.

Aside from, say, in England.

We want people to eat in restaurants that don't provide English menus. We don't like to see the United States when we're visiting Italy; we want foreign when we're on foreign soil. When we visited Athens we were horrified to see a gigantic neon-and-plastic, two-story Kenny Rogers Roast Chicken franchise on Syntagma Square right smack across from the Greek Parliament. On the beautiful port of Marigot on the island of St. Martin in the French West Indies, a single Kentucky Fried Chicken put all of the small, locally owned and picturesque grill shacks, called *lolos*, out of business, virtually destroying what was charming about the port. We have nothing against fast food, but when we're in Italy, we want it to look Italian. We don't want to see the golden arches near the Leaning Tower and we don't want to see a menu in English. As we see it, a menu in English is the first step in the Americanization of the restaurants of the world, the first domino. And once it's not foreign, what's the point of going?

~ ITALY ~

ABRUZZO & MOLISE
(Off-the-Beaten-Track Italy)

Along the Adriatic coast
are the mountainous
regions of Abruzzo and
Molise. The quiet hill towns
are in great contrast to the
Adriatic resorts. The most notable
tourist venue is the Abruzzo National
Park, a place for hikers and nature lovers.
Outside this nature reserve is Scanno, a
popular summer resort town. L`Aquila
(which means "the eagle") is the capital of Abruzzo and is a business center. Few tourists from the United
States and Canada visit this part of
Italy. If you're looking for off-the-
beaten-track destinations and mountain
scenery, Molise and Abruzzo will cer-
tainly please.

Inland, you will find menus dominated by *capretto* (baby goat),
agnello arrosto (roast lamb), and *porchetta* (roast pig). On the
coast (in restaurants not serving tourist fare) try *brodetto* (fish soup). *Centerbe* (a green herb liquor) accompa-
nies many meals. For dessert, try *confetti* (flower-
shaped candy made from sugar-coated almonds).

APULIA (The "Heel" of Italy)

Apulia (Puglia) is the "heel" of Italy. Oppressively hot in July and
August, a rainy day is rare. Apulia is a large wine-producing
region. The area is not frequented by many North American
tourists. The baroque town of Martina Franca and the whitewashed town of Locorotondo are in the wine region and worth a

visit. Part of the coast is heavily industrialized with immense steelworks. Bari is a modern port and a common departure point for travelers to Greece. *Trulli*, dome-shaped whitewashed stone buildings, are indigienous to the area. The largest collection of *trulli* can be found near Alberobello. The Adriatic fishing ports have architecture similar to the old Venetian ports. Taranto is a modern town, as is the important port of Brindisi, another frequent departure point for visits to Greece. Not to be missed is the lovely Baroque town of Lecce.

Focaccia barese (stuffed pizza), often with *burrata* (very buttery cheese), *triglia* (red mullet), *spigola* (sea bass), *orecchiette con le cime di rapa* (ear-shaped pasta with turnips) and *tiella di riso e cozze* (a mussels, rice and potato dish) can all be found on Apulia's menus. Some avoid the *polpi arricciati* ("curled octopus") when they see that the octopus is beaten and twirled in a basket in order to get the desired "curled" shape. *Bianco di Martina* is a common fortified wine found in Apulia.

BASILICATA (Undiscovered Italy)

This area was once known as Lucania. One of Italy's smallest regions, Basilicata is also its poorest. Mountainous and barren, Basilicata is not visited by many tourists. The capital city of Potenza was badly damaged in a 1980's earthquake. The hill town of Maratea is dramatically situated on the coast. Here, in small villages such as Metaponto and Matera, you experience the simple Italy.

Spicy *sugna piccante* (pork sauce) flavors many dishes. *Maiale* (pork) is found on most menus, and cured meats like

Friuli-Venezia Giulia

eneto

San Marino

Le Marche

Abruzzo

Molise

Apulia

Campania

Basilicata

Calabria

Sicily

the sausage *luganega*, *luganica* or *lucanica* (there are even more spellings than this!) are common. *Peperoncini* (small hot green peppers preserved in oil) are added to many dishes. Try *scamorza* cheese (the local version of aged *mozzarella*).

CALABRIA (The "Toe" of Italy)

Sun, white-sand beaches, rugged mountains, olive groves and the huge rock of Scilla are all found on the "toe" of Italy. The area was once known as Magna Graecia, and there are villages where a Greek dialect is still spoken. The mountain towns such as Serra San Bruno remain as they were several hundred years ago. Rossano is a beautiful medieval town overlooking a great ravine. Consenza is a town built on a steep hillside with an interesting (almost dilapidated) look to it. Many tourists find themselves in modern Reggio on their way to Sicily. The small towns of Pizzo and Tropea are worth a visit to experience the true Calabria. We would be remiss if we did not mention that some areas of Calabria are strongholds of the local mafia and not recommended for travel.

Costolette d'agnello (lamb chops) and *pesce spada* (swordfish) are found on most menus. *Novellame* is a spread of salted anchovies and *peperoncino* sauce. Pasta is often served with chickpeas (*ceci*). *Stracotto* is a beef stew which in Calabria includes carrots, mushrooms, onions, nutmeg and cloves. *Caviale del sud* or "caviar of the south" is a dish of fried fish preserved in oil and powdered with *peperoncino*. *Fichi* (figs) are featured in many desserts.

CAMPANIA (Naples, Capri & the Amalfi Coast)

Naples, in the shadow of Vesuvius, is congested, noisy, has a reputation as dangerous, and is not an easy city for the tourist. After a quick view of Naples' old town along the harbor, most head for the nearby ruins of Herculaneum and Pompeii. It's an eerie experience walking through nearly perfectly preserved ancient communities buried by the volcanic eruption of

Vesuvius. The volcanic island of Ischia and nearby Capri are often overrun by day trippers in high season.

Although it can be expensive, Capri (with its breathtaking vistas) remains the favorite of many returning visitors. The gateway to the Amalfi coast is Sorrento, perched over the sea. The Amalfi coast is the most spectacular coastal drive in Italy (if you have the nerve to drive it in high season). Positano has a great beach with a view of the town perched on the bluff. Amalfi and Ravello, further down the Amalfi coast, have spectacular views. The Amalfi coast reigns as one of the most scenic and photographed coasts in the world.

Seafood is prevalent along the coast, especially *polpi affogati* (octopus in a spicy tomato sauce). Pizza, said to have originated in Naples, is found in many varieties. *Pizza alla Napoletana* is pizza with tomato sauce and anchovies. You will eat tomatoes here like you have never had before. Many pasta dishes are served *al pomodoro* (with a tomato sauce). Meat is often cooked *alla pizzaiola* (in a tomato sauce with garlic). *Partenopea* on a menu simply means served Naples style. For dessert try *sfogliatella* (flaky pastry filled with sweet *ricotta* cheese).

EMILIA-ROMAGNA (From the Adriatic Sea to Central Italy)

The Romans built a grand road from Rimini on the Adriatic Sea to Piacenza in central Italy. The towns that now make up this region developed along this road, the Via Emilia. Piacenza is a major industrial city with a lovely downtown. Parma (which lends its name to the famous Parma ham or *prosciutto*), Modena (home to the Ferrari and Maserati automobiles), Bologna (a learning center, important city for commerce, and *the* food town in Italy), and Ferrara (less spoiled by modern times than the others) are all towns with important historic centers. Imposing Ravenna is in contrast to the most popular Adriatic resort of Rimini. Be careful, as Rimini can be quite dull, even completely closed, off season and extremely overcrowded in season.

The coast features *brodetto* (fish soup). *Prosciutto di Parma* (Parma ham) is common as is *risotto* (the famous Italian rice dish). Suckling pig is called *lattonzolo* here. For dessert, try *castagnole* (chestnut fritters). True Italian food is rare in Rimini, which has revised its menus to cater to the European package tourist.

FRIULI-VENEZIA GIULIA (Trieste & the Austrian Border)

This region borders on Austria and Slovenia. Udine is the capital but Trieste draws the most attention. Trieste, which remained under United Nations control until 1954, is an interesting mix of Austrian and Italian with a Slavic influence from the former Yugoslav republics. The architecture along the port demonstrates the mix of rulers in Trieste. Our several trips to Trieste have made us realize that this area is often, unfortunately, overlooked by tourists. White wine is produced in the hills of Friuli-Venezia Giulia. Visit the towns of Colli Orientali and Collio. The small mountain towns along the Austrian border allow the visitor to experience a mixture of Italy and Austria.

Jota is a minestrone found here and usually contains sauerkraut. *Polenta* (cornmeal mush) is found everywhere. *Brodetto* (fish soup) is common in the coastal area of this region. *Cialzons* is a sweet-and-sour pasta dish found here. The town of San Daniele is the home of *prosciutto di San Daniele* (a cured ham). The Slavic influence is found in the Trieste dessert of *gubana* (sweet bread roll) and the Austrian influence is found in the many coffeehouses of Trieste.

LAZIO (Rome & its Environs)

Lazio (also called Latium) is the region around Rome. To try to list Rome's main attractions would require another guide. Rome can be a frustrating city (it can be hard to carry on a conversation while walking down the street due to the constant traffic noise). But, difficulties aside, few places in the world have so many important sites in such a small area,

including the Vatican with its Sistine Chapel, Circus Maximus, the Spanish Steps, the Trevi Fountain, the catacombs...

Sperlonga, San Felice Circeo, Santa Severa and Santa Marinella are all coastal towns worth a visit. Ostia is a large coastal city near Rome and was the main Roman port. Its impressive ruins are an easy day trip from Rome. In inland Lazio, you may visit Tivoli (with Hadrian's Villa), Palestrina, the mountain town of Subiaco and the walled town of Viterbo.

Rome is said to have 5,000 restaurants where you can eat just about anything. After a grueling day of sightseeing, stop in a small restaurant (*trattoria*), drink some wine and eat a hearty dish of pasta such as one served *all' arrabbiata* (in a spicy tomato and herb sauce) or *alla carbonara* (with bacon, cheese, olive oil and eggs). Meals often start with *bruschetta* (garlic toast) and end with *grappa* (of which we drank a little too much on our first night here). When in Rome...

LE MARCHE (The Apennines Mountain Region)

The Apennines Mountains separate Le Marche from the rest of Central Italy. Ancona, on the Adriatic coast (a common departure point for Venice) is a modern port town. Pilgrims visit the house of the Virgin Mary in Loreto (brought here, according to legend, by angels). Urbino, one of the lesser-known great Renaissance cities, looks much as it did in the fifteenth century. In the Tronto River Valley, scenic Ascoli Piceno is another Le Marche town worth visiting. Most travelers head for the crowded (package tour-filled) coastal towns. These crowded resorts are in great contrast to the sedate hill towns.

Truffles (*tartufi*) are a specialty here, and summer peaches (*pesche*) and plums (*susine*) are some of the best fruits you will ever taste. *Vincigrassi* (baked lasagna dish), *olive all'ascolana* (large stuffed olives), *porchetta* (roast suckling pig) and rabbit (*coniglio*) are popular. *Brodetto di pesce* (fish soup) is found along the coast. In Ancona, *brodetto* contains thirteen varieties of fish.

LIGURIA (The Italian Riviera)

Wedged between mountains and the sea, the coastal region of Liguria stretches from the French border to Tuscany and is a popular tourist destination. Genoa, a large industrial city, is also Italy's biggest port. Tourists usually visit only the old, central part of the city. West of Genoa toward the French border are the bright tourist towns of Ventimiglia and Bordighera. San Remo (with its famous casino) is the largest resort. East from Genoa, you will find the resort of Nervi with beautiful parks. Further down the coast are the resort towns of Camogli, Rapallo, Santa Margherita and of course, perhaps the best known and most beautiful Italian port of Portofino. One drawback is the gridlock in and out of Portofino in high season. Sestri Levante makes a good base for exploring the highlight of any trip to Liguria, the Cinque Terre, five beautiful towns, which until recently were accessible only by train or a series of hiking paths. Perched on dramatic cliffs above the sea, you will experience car-free serenity and an Italy of old. Down the coast is Lerici (where we had one of our most memorable meals in an open-air restaurant on the port).

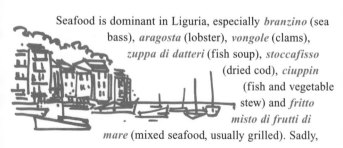

Seafood is dominant in Liguria, especially *branzino* (sea bass), *aragosta* (lobster), *vongole* (clams), *zuppa di datteri* (fish soup), *stoccafisso* (dried cod), *ciuppin* (fish and vegetable stew) and *fritto misto di frutti di mare* (mixed seafood, usually grilled). Sadly, seafood is becoming less common because of pollution and overfishing in the Mediterranean. *Basilico* (basil) grown in the hills above the sea forms the basis of *pesto* and is common in the cuisine of Liguria. Try *ravioli di magro* (pasta stuffed with herbs and *ricotta* cheese).

LOMBARDY (Milan & the Lake District)

Fashionable, modern Milan is an important center of Italian commerce. If you like to shop, Milan is the place. Tourists often visit four important sites: the Duomo (cathedral, especially the ornate roof), La Scala (the opera house), the Last Supper (at the church of Santa Maria delle Grazie), and the Galleria Vittorio Emanuele (the famous glass-domed shopping center).

In great contrast to Milan is the Lake District, including Lakes Orta (often, regrettably, ignored), Maggiore, Como, and Garda. The towns that line these lakes remain dotted with former palaces (many now resorts) with impressive formal gardens. Many believe the Lake District is Italy at its best. On Lake Como, Bellagio is the most famous resort, but Varenna, with its tiny harbor and splendid beach, is the favorite of many.

Trota (trout) is popular in the Lake District. Lombardy specialties include *stracotto* (pot roast), *ossobuco* (braised veal shank) and *capretto* (roast kid). You will find many dishes served *alla milanese* (battered with eggs and breadcrumbs and fried). *Risotto alla milanese* is a popular rice dish made golden from the ingredient saffron. *Gorgonzola* (a delicious blue cheese) is often found in pasta dishes. Lombardy cheeses also included *crescenza* (a soft, buttery cheese) and *mascarpone* (a very creamy cheese). *Torrone* (honey-and-almond nougat) is a common dessert.

Sometimes the Alpine regions of Piedmont (which means "foot of the mountain") and Valle d'Aosta (north of Piedmont) feel more like France or Switzerland than Italy. Valle d'Aosta has two official languages: Italian and French. Many come to the largest city in these regions, Turin (Torino), to see the Shroud of Turin (believed by some to be the cloth in which Christ's body was wrapped after the crucifixion). North of Turin, into Valle d'Aosta, is Saint Vincent (a popular gambling resort). Any trip to this area would not be complete without a visit to Breuil-Cervina at the base of the Matterhorn (Monte Cervino) with breathtaking views of this famous mountain peak. Courmayeur, another Alpine resort, is the gateway to Mont Blanc (Monte Bianco) on the French border. The walled city of Aosta is nestled in the Alps. Asti (yes, as in the wine), Novara, Vercelli, and Casale Monferrato are all towns with impressive medieval towers. If you're looking for beautiful mountain scenery, don't miss these regions.

Piemontese on a menu means "Piedmont style" or with white truffles. *Tartufi bianchi* are famous white truffles from Alba and Asti. *Alla Valdostana* on a menu means "Valle d'Aosta style" and usually means with ham and cheese. Roast game, sausages and butter play heavy roles in the local diet. *Tajarin* is thin ribbon pasta made golden with egg yolks. *Fonduta* (fondue) is popular. The French influence can be found in *crespelle* (crêpes). You will find *cervo* (venison), *carbonade* (beef cooked in wine and onions) and *arrosto misto* (grilled meats) here along with *trota* (trout). *Gianduiotti* are hazelnut chocolates found in Turin and one of our favorite treats. *Torta di nocciole*, hazelnut cake, is a must.

With about only 25,000 people and 24 square miles, San Marino (totally surrounded by Italy) claims to be Europe's oldest existing country. San Marino's official name is the Most Serene Republic of San Marino, and is located 15 miles inland from the Adriatic Sea resort of Rimini. Its chief industries are tourism and the sale of postage stamps. Mt. Titano, upon which San Marino sits, must be climbed after you leave your car. There are three medieval fortresses on the mountain. The capital, also named San Marino, is a maze of attractive narrow streets.

Food is typical Italian. You'll find *coniglio* (rabbit) and *nidi di rondine* (pasta rolls). Don't miss *caciatella* (San Marino's version of crème caramel).

SARDINIA (SARDEGNA)

The island of Sardinia is located about 115 miles off the western coast of Italy in the Mediterranean. Ten miles to the north is the French island of Corsica. Sardinia has been a part of Italy since 1861. Cagliari, the capital, is on the south coast, which is known for its ancient ruins. For the most part, Sardinia remains unspoiled from its rocky coast to its mountainous interior. The northeastern Costa Smeralda (Emerald Coast) is the only area where tourist development has arrived. Those looking for peace and quiet and even isolation should experience the mountainous inland region of Barbagia.

Lobster (*aragosta*) is plentiful along the coast, and the northern coast of Sardinia is sometimes referred to as the lobster coast. Lamb (*agnello*), rabbit (*cunillu*) and trout (*trota*) are ubiquitous. Grilled meats are a specialty. The shepherds of Sardinia feast on *pane carasau*, which is also known as *carta da musica* (music paper). Durham wheat, salt, water and yeast are the simple ingredients for this wood fire-baked bread. You will find this thin, crispy bread used as a pizza crust.

Other specialties of Sardinia include *porceddu* (roast suckling pig, which is the "national" dish of Sardinia), *cascà* (couscous), and many honey-based desserts such as *sebadas* (deep-fried cheese-filled ravioli soaked in honey).

SICILY (SICILIA)

French, Arabs, Spanish and Italians have all controlled Sicily, the largest and most populated island in the Mediterranean. Travelers will find some of the best-preserved Greek and Roman ruins here, along with the ornate architecture of its churches and palaces. Agrigento is home to the most important archaeological site in Sicily, the Greek "Valley of the Temples." Siracusa (Syracuse) is also known for its Greek and Roman ruins. The capital is Palermo, but most travelers head to the medieval town of Taormina on the east coast in the shadows of Mount Etna, an active volcano. Messina (destroyed by both an earthquake and the bombs of World War II) has bland, modern architecture, and is in strong contrast to the picturesque fishing port of Cefalù.

Sicilian cuisine is not simply pasta and olive oil but incorporates Italian, Greek, French, Spanish and Arab influences. Some specialties are *pasta con le sarde* (pasta with fresh sardines), *pesce spada* (swordfish), and the simple *cicina* (a mixture of fried small fish).

Other specialties are *caponata* (sweet-and-sour sauce with eggplant, tomatoes, onions and peppers), *pasta alla Norma* (pasta with a tomato, basil and eggplant sauce topped with *ricotta* cheese) and *costoletta alla siciliana* (thin slices of veal or beef topped with chopped garlic and *parmesan* cheese, then breaded and deep-fried).

Desserts, and Sicilians

are famous for their desserts, include *cannoli* (pastry tubes filled with sweetened *ricotta* cheese) and *cassata alla siciliana* (layered spongecake).

Marsala wine (from the town of the same name) is a fortified wine that can range from rich and sweet to dry.

TICINO (Italian-Speaking Switzerland)

Ticino is the main Italian-speaking canton or region of Switzerland. Palm trees, Italian architecture, Swiss orderliness and Italian food all make Ticino (with its famous resorts of Lugano and Locarno) a great travel destination. Ticino is Switzerland's southernmost canton, bordering on Italy, and has been a part of Switzerland since the early 1800s. This region has always remained strongly Italian. Italian is one of four official languages of Switzerland (along with French, German and Romansh).

Specialties found in Ticino are *risotto ai fiori di zucca* (a rice dish made with a heavy cream base and zucchini flowers stirred in along with *parmesan* cheese), *pancetta arrotolata* (rolled bacon flavored with cloves), *capretto* (baby goat), *fritto misto* (breaded and fried lake fish), *cotto antico* (bay leaf-flavored salami), and *giambonetti di pollo* (stuffed chicken leg). Bread is a staple in all meals, especially bread with a thick crust dusted with flour called *crusca*. Two common cheeses found in Ticino are *formaggini di capra* (fresh goat's-milk cheese) and *formaggini d'Alpe* (a common cow's-milk cheese). Both of these cheeses are eaten with olive oil, salt and pepper.

TRENTINO-ALTO ADIGE (The Dolomites)

The Alto Adige is the far north of Italy and is more like Austria than Italy. The Dolomite Mountains dominate this area. At the Brenner Pass, on the border with Austria, is the town of Bolzano/Bozen (Austrian until 1918). Near Bolzano is the wine town of Caldaro. Bressanone/Brixen is a beautiful mountain town and the Alto Adige's oldest city. Ortisei, San Martino and Madonna di Campiglio are all summer and winter resort towns. Breathtaking views abound in Brunico/Bruneck. Merano has an interesting old town and famous spas. Trento, the capital of Trentino, is more Italian than Austrian and remains an attractive an architecturally interesting town.

Food here is more German than Italian (especially the farther north you travel). Game, dumplings (*knoedel*) and cured ham (*speck*) all stress the German influence. Sauerkraut (*crauti*) is featured heavily in dishes, as are *wurstel* (hot dogs and brats). For dessert, apples, grown in large numbers in the region, are often added to the Germanic dessert of *strudel*.

TUSCANY (One of the World's Most Popular Destinations)

There are so many picturesque towns in Tuscany, space allows only a few highlights. With unspoiled hills, perfectly preserved towns and great food and wine, Tuscany is one of the most popular tourist destinations in Italy and the world. Since childhood, we wanted to see the Leaning Tower of Pisa (and the nearby and lesser-known baptistery). Too bad there are so many hawkers of plastic leaning towers all over Pisa. Siena's main square, the Piazza del Campo, and ornate cathedral are only two gems in the beautiful town with (thankfully) a car-free center. San Gimignano, with its walls and towers, is an incredibly picturesque town. The hilltop towns of Lucca, Montepulciano, Montalcino and Pienza are all worth a visit. Of course, Florence is the favorite of many visitors to Italy. Its wealth of art, housed in buildings which themselves are art, leaves many visitors wanting to return again and again.

Start your meal with *crostini* (toasted bread with various toppings). *La bistecca alla Fiorentina*, a T-bone steak, must not be missed, nor should any of the *pecorino* cheeses. Menus often include dishes served *alla lepre* (in a rabbit-based sauce), *cinghiale* (wild boar), *arista* (roast, seasoned pork loin), and *ribollita* (bean and/or cabbage soup which means "twice-cooked soup). *Chianti, chianti* and more *chianti*. Enough said!

UMBRIA (Assisi & the Hill Towns North of Rome)

Green hills, towns spared from industrialization, and wonderful dining combine to make Umbria an outstanding Italian destination (especially by car). Perugia is Umbria's largest city with a historic city center, but most tourists come here to visit the smaller towns like Gubbio in northern Umbria. Orvieto is located on a monumental square-shaped rock visible for miles. Don't miss this impressive and well-preserved town (or a taste of its famous wines). Assisi is home to a huge basilica built in memory of local hero St. Francis. It's ironic that such a huge basilica was built for such a humble man, or that the streets are filled with shops selling St. Francis keychains. Still, Assisi, perched on a hill, is a memorable sight. Walled Spoleto (home of the well-known art festival) is dominated by a large castle and is surrounded by wooded countryside.

Tartufi (truffles) are a specialty here, especially the black truffle (*tartufo nero*). *Stringozzi* (homemade pasta) is used in many dishes, especially in Spoleto. *Strozzapreti* (dumplings with meat sauce) is a dish with the strange name of "priest stranglers" after a priest allegedly choked on it. *Palombacci* are small songbirds cooked whole on a spit. For dessert, try *stinchetti* (marzipan cakes). Of course, no one thinks of eating in Umbria without drinking one of the many fine wines of this region.

VENETO (Venice & its Environs)

Veneto is the region around Venice. Despite the tourists, the sometimes smelly canals and the often

inflated prices, Venice is unlike anywhere else in the world. Many cities claim to be pedestrian only, but Venice is truly car-free. Don just take a day trip here. Once the day trippers leave, Venice becomes a quiet, romantic maze of streets wi spectacular architecture. As many times as we have visited, we a always amazed at the splendid beauty of Venice with its building rising out of the sea. Don't miss the Piazza San Marco, the Bridg of Sighs, the Basilica di San Marco and the Doge's Palace. If tim permits, visit the islands of Murano (famous for its ornate glass) Burano (famous for its lace), San Michele (Venice's island ceme tery) and Torcello (for a taste of an almost deserted island).

Veneto includes the cities of Vicenza, Padua (where you can see the "uncorrupted" tongue of St. Anthony), Verona and Treviso. Many towns remain unspoiled and rarely visited by tourists, including Valpolicella (home of this popular Italian red wine), the hills of Colli Euganei (home of hot thermal springs), and Asolo. North of Treviso are the mountain resorts of Cortina d' Ampezzo and Belluno.

Cape sante (scallops), *baccalà* (dried cod), *fegato alla veneziana* (liver with onions), *seppie* (cuttle-fish), and *granseola* (crab) are all specialties of Venice. *Polenta* (the famous cornmeal mush) is found throughout the region. *Carpaccio* is thinly sliced raw beef served in a sauce, and was named by the owner of Harry's Bar in Venice after a famous Venetian painter. *Prosecco* is a slightly sparkling wine from Veneto and worth a try. While in Venice, don't miss having an evening drink or *caffè* in the Piazza San Marco.

Speaking Italian - Pronunciation Guide

If you're looking for a comprehensive guide to speaking Italian, this is not the the place. These are simply a few tips for speaking Italian followed by a very brief pronunciation guide. It's always good to learn a few polite terms so that you can excuse yourself when you've stepped on the foot of an elderly lady or spilled your drink down the back of the gentleman in front of you. It's also just common courtesy to greet the people you meet in your hotel, and in shops and restaurants, in their own language.

In Italian, you pronounce every letter. E and i are soft vowels when used with consonants. The final e is always pronounced.

The second to the last syllable is stressed. If there is an accent in the word, stress the accented syllable.

a like in father.
au like ow in cow.
b the same as in English.
c **ca, co** and **cu** like k in keep.
– **ce** and **ci**, like ch in cheap.
ch like k in kite.
d the same as in English.
e like in day.
ei like ay in lay.
f the same as in English.
g **ga, go** and **gu** like g in gate.
– **ge** and **gi** like j in jar.
gh like g in goat.
gl like gl in glow except before i, then like lli in million.
gn like ni in onion.
h silent. H after a consonant gives it a hard sound.
i like ee in jeep.
ie, io, iu, **i** is pronounced as y (ie. *pensione* ~ pen syo neh).
k/l/m/n the same as in English.
o usually like o in boat.

p/q the same as in English.
ue, ui, uo, the u is pronounced like a w (ie. *buono* ~ bwo no).
r with a slight trill.
s like s in sit except between two vowels, then like s in hose.
sc **sca, sco** or **scu** as sk in skirt.
– **sce** or **sci** as sh in sharp.
t the same as English.
u like oo in foot.
v the same as in English.
z the same as ds in fads.

Pronunciation

CA – KA
CE – CHAY
CI – CHEE
CHI – KEY
CHE –KAY

Confused?

This is a brief listing of some familiar English food and food-related words that you may need in a restaurant, followed by a list of phrases that may come in handy.

anchovy, acciuga (acciughe)
appetizer, antipasto (i)
apple, mela (e)
artichoke, carciofo (i)
ashtray, portacenere
asparagus, asparago (i)
bacon, pancetta
baked, al forno
banana, banana (e)
bean, fagiolo (i)
beef, manzo (di bue)
beefsteak, bistecca (di manzo)
beer, birra (e)
beverage, bevanda (e)
bill, conto (i)
bitter, amaro (a)
boiled, bollito/lesso
bottle, bottiglia
bowl, scodella
bread, pane
bread rolls, panino (i)
breakfast, prima colazione
broiled, graticola/griglia
broth, brodo
butter, burro
cabbage, cavolo (i)
cake, torta (e)
candle, candela
carrot, carota (e)
cereal, cereale (i)
chair, sedia

Words that end in A or O are singular

Words that end in E or I are plural

Carciofo ~ car CHEE OH FO

bottiglia ~ bow·tee·Lee-ah

Words and letters in parentheses indicate plurals.

cereale ~ cheer·ee·ah-LaY

check, conto (i)

cheers, salute/cin cin

cheese, formaggio (formaggi)

cherry, ciliegia (e)

chicken soup, brodo di pollo/zuppa di pollo

chicken, pollo

chop, costoletta (e)

clam, vongola (e)

cocktail, cocktail

cod, baccalà/merluzzo

coffee, caffè (also black coffee)

**coffee w/hot water
   (to dilute),** caffè amercano

coffee w/milk, caffè latte

coffee (decaf), caffè hag/caffè decaffeinato

coffee w/cream, caffè con panna

cold, freddo (a)

corn, mais

cover charge, pane coperto

cucumber, cetriolo (i)

cup, coppa

   tazza coffee/tea cup

custard, crema

dessert, dolce (i)

dinner, cena

dish (plate), piatto

drink, bevanda (e)

dry (as in wine), secco

duck, anitra/anatra

egg, uovo (a)

espresso, caffè espresso

fish, pesce

fish soup, zuppa di pesce

fork, forchetta

french fries, patate fritte

fresh, fresco (a)

fried, fritto (a)/fritti (e)

caffè italiano.

caffè americano.

freddo ~
FRAY-doh

dolce ~
dole-chay

cena ~
chain-ah

forchetta.

forchetta ~
FOR-KAY-TAH

fruit, frutta
game, cacciagione/selvaggina
garlic, aglio
gin, gin
glass, bicchiere
grapefruit, pompelmo
grape, uva
green bean, fagiolino (i)
grilled, griglia or alla griglia
half, mezzo (a)
ham (cooked), prosciutto cotto
ham (cured), prosciutto crudo
hamburger, hamburger
honey, miele
hors d'oeuvre, antipasto
hot, caldo (a)
iced, ghiacciato
ice coffee, caffè freddo
ice cream, gelato (i)
ice (on the rocks), ghiaccio or con ghiaccio
ice water, acqua fredda
iced tea, tè freddo
ketchup, ketchup/salsa di pomodoro
knife, coltello
lamb, abbacchio/agnello
large, grande
lemon, limone (i)
lettuce, lattuga
little (a little), un pó
liver, fegato (fegatini)
lobster, aragosta (e)
loin, lombata
lunch, pranzo
marinated, marinato (a)
match, fiammifero (i)
meat, carne
medium (cooked), a puntino or normale

Bicchiere.
BEE·KEE·AY·RAY

griglia
GREE-LEE·AH

ghiacciato ~
ghee-AH-chee-A·TOE

coltello.

melon, melone
menu, carta or menù
milk, latte
mineral water, acqua minerale
mineral water (sparkling), acqua minerale gasata
mineral water (w/out carbonation), acqua minerale non gasata
mixed, mista (o)
mushroom, fungo (i)
mussel, cozza (e)
mustard, senape
napkin, tovagliolo
noodles, taglierini/pasta
octopus, polipo/polpo
oil, olio
olive oil, olio d'oliva
omelette, frittata
on the rocks (w/ ice), con ghiaccio
onion, cipolla (e)
orange, arancia (arance)
orange juice, succo d'arancia
overdone, ben cotto
oyster, ostrica (ostriche)
pastries, dolci/paste
peach, pesca (pesche)
pear, pera (e)
pea, pisello (i)
pepper (black), pepe
pepper (bell), peperone (i)
perch, pesce persico
pineapple, ananas
plate (dish), piatto
please, per piacere
plum, susina (e)
poached, affogato
pork, maiale

funghi.

Tovagliolo ~
Toe·vah·Lee·oh·Lo

Cipolla ~
chee·poLLa

per piacere ~
pare-pee·ah·chair·AY

maiale ~
my·AL·LAY

31

potato, patata (e)
poultry, pollame
prawn, gamberetto (i)
rabbit, coniglio
rare, al sangue
raspberry, lampone (i)
receipt, ricevuta/scontrino
rice, riso
roast, arrosto
salad, insalata
salt, sale
sandwich, sandwich/panino (i)
sauce, salsa
saucer, piattino/sottocoppa
sautéed, saltato (i)/saltata (e)
scallops, cappe sante
scrambled, strapazzate
seafood, frutti di mare
seasoning, condimento (i)
shrimp, scampo (i),
    gamberetto (i)
small, piccolo (i)/piccola (e)
smoked, affumicata (o)
snail, lumaca (lumache)
sole, sogliola (e)
soup, zuppa (e)/minestra (e)
spaghetti, spaghetti
sparkling wine, spumante
specialty, specialità
spinach, spinaci
spoon, cucchiaio
squid, calamaro (i)
steak, bistecca
steamed, a vapore
stewed, in umido
strawberry, fragola (e)
sugar, zucchero

Coniglio.
Co-NEE-LEO

ricevuta ~
ree-chay-voo-tah

gamberetto.

Lumaca.

spaghetti ~
spa-get-tee

cucchiaio ~
KOO KEE AYE OH

zucchero ~
zoo-KARE-oH

sugar substitute, dolcificante

supper, cena

sweet, dolce *dolce* – DOL-CHAY

table, tavolo

tea, tè

tea w/lemon, tè al limone

tea w/milk, tè al latte TAZZA di tè.

teaspoon, cucchiaino

thank you, grazie

tip, mancia

toasted, tostato

tomato, pomodoro (i)

trout, trota

tumbler (glass), bicchiere

tuna, tonno *tacchino*

turkey, tacchino TA-KEE-NO

utensil, posata (e)/utensile (i)

veal, vitello

veal scallop, scaloppa di vitello

vegetable, legume (i). *Verdura (e)* green vegetables

vegetarian, vegetariana (o)

venison, carne di cervo

vinegar, aceto

waiter, cameriere

waitress, cameriera

water, acqua

well done, ben cotto

whipped cream, panna montata

wine, vino

wine (full-bodied), vino corposo

wine list, lista dei vini

wine (red), vino rosso

wine (rosé), vino rosé

wine (white), vino bianco

Unless there's a written translation, it pretty much sounds like it looks, only more Italian sounding. Don't forget to pronounce that final 'E'!

Helpful Phrases

Prego can mean: thank you, you're welcome, this way (with a hand gesture), please, okay, and can I help you.

Ciao means hello *and* goodbye.

Italians answer the phone with *Pronto?*

please, per piacere/per favore
thank you, grazie
yes, sì
no, no
good morning, buon giorno
good afternoon/evening, buona sera
good night, buona notte
goodbye, arrivederci/ciao
do you speak English?, parla inglese?
I don't speak Italian, non parlo italiano
excuse me, mi scusi (or *scusi*)
I don't understand, non capisco
I'm hungry, Ho fame
I'm thirsty, Ho sete
I'd like..., Vorrei...
I'd like a table, please, Vorrei un tavolo, per piacere
I want to reserve a table, Vorrei prenotare un tavolo
for one person, per uno (una)
for two persons, per due
   tre (3)
   quattro (4)
   cinque (5)
   sei (6)
   sette (7)
   otto (8)
   nove (9),
   dieci (10)
this evening, stasera
tomorrow, domani

Handwritten annotations:

non is pronounced almost like NONG.

Ho fame ~ OH fah·may

Ho sete OH - SETTAY

OONO
DOO AY
TRAY
KWATRO
CHINK·WAY
SAY
SET·TAY
OH TOe
NO VAY
dee AY CHI

34

the day after tomorrow, dopodomani

near the window, vicino alla finestra

vicino ~
VEE CHEE NO

outside, fuori

fuori ~
FOO oH REE

inside, dentro

on the patio, sulla veranda

no smoking, zona per non fumatori. Since 2005, Italian law bans
   smoking in public places, including bars and restaurants

where is?, dov'è

the bathroom, il bagno/la toilette

the bill please, il conto, per piacere

a mistake, errore

is service included?, é incluso il servizio?

do you accept credit cards?, Posso pagare con una carta di credito?

how much does this cost?, quanto costa?

what is this?, cos' è questo?

this is not what I ordered, non ho ordinato questo

this is, questo è...

too, troppo

a little, un po'

cold, freddo (a)

freddo ~
FRAY-doh

hot, caldo (a)

spicy, piccante

not fresh, non è fresco

undercooked, troppo crudo

overcooked, troppo cotto/stracotto

very good, molto buono

delicious, delizioso (a)

diet, dieta

allergic, allergico (a)

closed, chiuso (a)

chiuso ~
KEE-YOU-ZO

Monday, lunedì

Tuesday, martedì

Wednesday, mercoledì

Thursday, giovedì

Friday, venerdì

Saturday, sabato

Sunday, domenica

abbacchio, lamb
abbacchio alla cacciatora, pieces of lamb braised w/rosemary, garlic, wine & peppers
abbacchio alla romana, pieces of lamb cooked until brown, then roasted in a rosemary, garlic, vinegar & anchovy sauce
abbacchio brodettato, pieces of lamb cooked in a broth of lemon, parsley & beaten eggs
abboccatto, a medium-sweet wine
abbrustolito, toasted
abruzzese, red pepper sauce
acciuga (acciughe), anchovy

acciuga ~ AH·CHEE·oo·ga

acciughe al limone, anchovies w/lemon-based sauce
acerbo, sour
aceto, vinegar
aceto balsamico, balsamic vinegar. Aged vinegar used in many dishes, especially salads
acetosella, sorrel
acido, sour
acini di pepe, pasta for soup in the shape of peppercorns
acqua, water
acqua brillante, tonic water
acquacotta, bread & vegetable soup
acquadella, small whitebait fish

"Acqua cotta" means cooked water

acqua di rubinetto, tap water
acqua di seltz, seltzer water/soda water
acqua fredda, ice water
acqua gasata, carbonated water
acqua ghiacciata, ice water
acqua minerale, mineral water
acqua minerale frizzante, extremely carbonated water
acqua minerale naturale, mineral water w/out carbonation
acqua naturale, tap water
acqua non gasata, water w/out carbonation
acqua non potabile, do not drink the water!
acqua pazza, sauce of tomato, garlic, oil, parsley & chili peppe
acqua semplice, tap water
acqua tonica, tonic water
Acquavite, brandy/distilled spirit flavored w/caraway
affettato, sliced

affettato (i), cold cut
affogato, poached. This can also refer
    to ice cream soaked in
    coffee or liqueur
affumicato, smoked
agliata/all'aglio, garlic sauce
aglio, garlic
aglio e olio, w/garlic & olive oil
agnello, lamb

Aglio.

agnello alla turca, lamb stew w/raisins
agnello con salsa di uovo, lamb w/egg
    sauce. A specialty in Le Marche
agnolotti, filled pasta (square shaped)
agone, freshwater fish found in the lake country
    (the size of sardines)
agresto, juice of unripened grapes
agro, lemon juice & olive oil dressing
agrodolce, sweet & sour sauce
ai/al/all'/alla, in the style of/with
ajula, sea bream
ala, wing
alaccia, large sardine
alalunga, albacore (a type of tuna)

Agresto is sometimes used in place of vinegar

Albana, dry to semi-sweet wine from Emilia-Romagna
albicocca (albicocche), apricot
albume, egg white
alcolica, alcoholic. *Una bevanda alcolica* is an alcoholic beverage
alcool, alcol
Aleatico, dessert wine (made from muscat grapes)
alette, wing
alfabetini, alphabet noodles for soup
al forno, baked
alfredo, w/butter & cream sauce
al fresco, outside (in the fresh air)
alice (i), anchovy
allodola (e), lark
alloro, bay leaf
amabile, slightly sweet wine
amarena (e), sour cherry
amaretti, macaroons
amaretto, sweet almond-flavored liqueur
amaro, bitter/bitter cordial (bitters)
amatriciana, bacon, tomato & spices sauce

ALLORO.

amburghese/amburgo, hamburger/ground meat

amburghese alla tirolese, hamburger served w/onion rings

Americano, Campari, vermouth & lemon peel

ammiru, prawns in Sicily

analcolico (i), non-alcoholic

ananas, pineapple

anatra, duck

anatroccolo, duckling

anelli/anellini, small circular
pasta for soup (ring pasta)

aneto, dill

anguidda, another name for eel in Sicily

anguilla (e), eel

anguilla alla veneziana, eel braised
w/tuna & lemon sauce

anguria, watermelon

anice, anise

animelle, sweetbreads

animelle alla salvia, sweetbreads w/sage

anisetta, anise-flavored liquor

anitra, duck

anitra germano, mallard duck

anitra selvatica, wild duck

annegati, slices of meat in wine

antipasto (i), appetizer

**antipasto alla marinara/antipasto di mare/antipasto di
pesce,** assorted seafood

antipasto misto, assorted appetizers

aperitivo, aperitif

arachide (i), peanut

aragosta (e), lobster (crayfish)

arancia (e), orange. *All' arancia* means w/orange juice

aranciata, orangeade/orange soda

arancini, deep-fried rice balls

arancio di riso, cooked ball of rice stuffed w/meat & breaded
& fried. This gets its name from the orange size of the ball

argentina, argentine fish

arigusta, crawfish

aringa, herring

aringa affumicata, smoked herring

arista, roast, seasoned pork loin

arista alla fiorentina, roasted pork rubbed w/garlic paste,
cloves, salt, rosemary, pepper

In Perugia Anguilla can also refer to an eel shaped pastry created originally by nuns.

arista di maiale/arista di suino, pork loin

arrabbiata, all', w/a spicy tomato & herb sauce

arrostetti, small roast

arrosti misti freddi, a selection of cold roasted meats

arrostini, veal chops

arrostino, small roast

arrostino annegato, small veal roast
  served with mushrooms

arrostite, grilled/roasted

arrosto/arrostito, roast/roasted

arrosto alla genovese, a roast w/onions, mushrooms
  & tomatoes

arrosto alla montanara, pot roast

arrosto con pastine, roast w/dough crust

arrosto di manzo, roast beef

arrosto in porchetta, roast suckling pig stuffed w/garlic,
  bacon & herbs

arrosto misto, mixed roast meats

arrosto morto, pot roast

arsella (e), mussel

asciutta (o), dry. Also refers to pasta w/sauce
  (as opposed to pasta for soup)

asiago, sharp cheese (round-shaped cheese)

asiago dolce, mild *asiago*

asparago (i), asparagus

asparago alla bismark, asparagus w/melted butter & fried egg

asparago alla milanese/asparago all'uovo, asaparagus topped
  w/melted butter, *parmesan* cheese & fried egg

assortito (i), assorted

astice (i), prawn/lobster

Asti Spumante, sparkling white wine

attorta, fruit- & almond-filled pastry

Aurum, orange liqueur

avvoltino, standing roast or rolled roast

babà, spongecake covered w/rum

babaluci, snails in tomato & onion sauce

bacca (e), berry

baccalà, salt cod

ASTI.

baccalà alla fiorentina, salt cod floured & fried in oil
  & tomato sauce

baccalà alla lucana, salt cod cooked w/peppers

baccalà alla vicentina, salt cod w/onion, parsley, garlic,
  anchovies & cinnamon

bacio, chocolate hazelnut (means "kiss")

bagna cauda/bagna caoda, hot vegetable dip w/anchovies

bagnet, sauce (in Piedmont)

balsamella, bechamel/white sauce

banana (e), banana   *Good Guess!*

bar, serves espresso, cappuccino, rolls, small sandwiches, alcoholic beverages and soft drinks

barbabietola (e), beet

Barbaresco, soft red wine from Piedmont (lighter & drier than *Barolo*)

Barbera, dry red wine

barbe rosse, beets

Bardolino, pale, light red wine

Barolo, rich red wine from Piedmont

Andy hates beets even in Italy.

basilico, basil

bastoncini, bread sticks (means "little sticks")

battuta scanello, pounded round steak

battutina al prosciutto, hamburger mixed w/cured ham

battuto, finely chopped herbs, onions, celery & carrots

battuto di manzo, ground beef

bavette (i), thin, flat pasta

beccaccia, woodcock

beccaccino, snipe (game)

beccafico, warbler/song bird

belga, Belgian endive

bellini, *Prosecco* & peach juice. Try one at Harry's Bar in Venice

bel paese, smooth, mild & soft cheese

ben cotta, well done

bensone, lemon cake

besciamella, white cream sauce

"Bel Paese" means beautiful country

bevanda (e), drink/beverage

bevanda compresa, cost of drinks included

bianchetti, small anchovy (or sardine)

bianchi, white

bianco, white wine

Bianco di Martina, a fortified wine found in Apulia

bianco, in, w/butter (w/out a sauce)

bibita (e), drink/beverage

bibite analcoliche, soft drinks

bicchiere, glass

biete, Swiss chard

bietole, beet/Swiss chard

Bicchiere.

BEE·KEE·AY·RAY

bietole alla padella, Swiss chard cooked w/butter &/or oil
bietoline, beet greens
bietolini, Swiss chard
bignè/bignole (con crema), cream puff
bigoli, larger form of spaghetti
biova/biovetta, round bread loaf
birra, beer
birra alla spina, tap beer
birra analcolica, no-alcohol beer
birra bionda, light beer
birra chiara, light beer (lager)
birra di barile, draft beer
birra importata, imported beer
birra in bottiglia, bottled beer

BiRRA

birra in lattina, beer in a can
birra scura, dark beer
biscotto (i), cookie/biscuit/cracker/spongecake
biscotti di prato, cookies w/pieces of almond
biscuit tortoni, dessert of beaten egg whites & macaroon
   crumbs topped w/whipped cream & toasted almonds
bismark, alla, usually means served w/a fried egg
bistecca, steak
bistecca alla bismark, fried steak w/an egg on top
bistecca alla fiorentina, T-bone steak
bistecca alla pizzaiola, steak w/tomato & garlic sauce
bistecca di manzo, beef steak
bistecca di vitello, veal scallop
bistecca Fiorentina, T-bone steak
bistecca impanata, cutlet/chop
bistecche, steaks
bistecchine, thin steaks
bitto, firm, smoked cheese
bobe, sea bream
boccolotti, short tubular pasta
bocconcini, diced veal w/tomato
   & white wine sauce/*mozzarella* balls
boldro, monkfish in Tuscany
boletus, porcini mushrooms
bollito (i), boiled. Can also mean meat or fish stew
bollito di gallina, boiled chicken
bollito di manzo, boiled beef
bollito misto, mixed boiled meats
bolognese, alla, usually means a tomato & meat sauce

Bistecca Impanata is often breaded and fried in butter

"bocconcini" means mouthful

bomba di riso, rice dish w/ground meat & herb fillings
bombolone (i), doughnut
bonèt, chocolate cream dessert. A specialty in Piedmont
borlotti, type of bean
boscaiola, means "woodsman style" & can refer to many
    things, including w/wild mushrooms
bosega, mullet
botolo, mullet
bottarga, fish eggs (tuna roe that has been salted & pressed)
bottiglia, bottle
bove, beef
bovoletti/bovoloni, small snails in Venice
brace, alla, on charcoal
braciola (e), rib steak/chop/cutlet
braciola di maiale, pork chop
bracioletta, small slice of meat
bracioletta a scottadito, lamb chops (charcoal grilled)
bracioline/braciolone, meat roll
braciolone alla napoletana, breaded steak, rolled & stewed
brandy, brandy
branzino, bass
branzinotti, small sea bass
brasato, braised/braised meat w/wine
bresaola, thinly sliced cured raw beef
briciole di pane, breadcrumbs
brioche, buns/rolls/small loaf (used for breakfast)
broccoletti, broccoli
broccoletti di rape, turnip greens
broccoletti strascinati, broccoli sautéed w/garlic & bacon
broccolo (i), broccoli
brodetto, rich fish soup
brodo, broth/soup/bouillon.
    In brodo means cooked in broth
brodo di manzo, consomme/beef broth
brodo di pollo, chicken soup
brogue, sea bream
brovada, marinated turnips w/pork sausage
Brunello, full-bodied red wine from Montalcino
bruschetta, grilled bread w/garlic & olive oil (frequently
    topped w/tomatoes &/or onions)
brut, very dry wine
brutti, small almond cakes
bucaniera, tomato & garlic seafood sauce

[handwritten margin notes: bottiglia ~ / Bow-Tee-Lee AH / Broccolo. / Bucaniera... / Buccaneer, / get it?]

42

bucatini, hollow spaghetti noodles
bucatoni, same as *bucatini*, but larger
budino, custard/pudding
budino alla toscana, cream cheese w/raisins, almonds,
    sugar & egg yolks
bue, beef
burrata, a very buttery cheese found in Apulia
burrida, fish stew or casserole. In Sardinia this refers to a
    poached & marinated fish dish
burrini, a type of hard, aged cheese
burro, butter
burro maggiordomo, butter w/lemon
    juice & parsley
busecca, tripe & vegetable soup
buttiri, a type of hard, aged cheese
cacao, cocoa
cacasor cioccolata, cocoa
cacciagione, game
cacciatora, alla/cacciatore, w/mushrooms,
    wine, tomatoes & herbs
cacciucco, spicy fish soup
cachi, persimmons
caciatella, a crème caramel dessert
cacio, *pecorino* cheese
caciocavallo, a hard, aged cheese
    made of whole milk
cacio e pepe, sauce made of
    black pepper & *pecorino* cheese
cacio e uova, w/cheese & egg
caciotta, mild cheese
caciucco, fish soup
caffè, coffee
caffè al vetro, coffee served in a glass
caffè americano, American-style coffee (Italian coffee diluted
    w/hot water)
caffè con panna, coffee w/cream
caffè corretto, *espresso* w/a shot of liquor (usually brandy)
caffè doppio, coffee (a double serving)
caffè espresso, *espresso*
caffè freddo, iced coffee
caffè hag, decaffeinated coffee
caffè latte, coffee w/steamed milk
caffè lungo, coffee w/water (weaker coffee)

[handwritten note:] alla cacciatora means in the style of the hunter

[handwritten note:] Traditionally there must be as many types of fish in the soup as c's in cacciucco.

caffè macchiato, coffee w/a small amount of warm milk
caffè nero, black coffee
caffè ristretto, small, thick & strong
   coffee (stronger than an *espresso*)
calamaretto (i), small squid
calamari, squid
calamari fritti, fried squid
calamito, grey mullet
caldo (a)/caldi (e), warm or hot
caldaro, fish & potato soup
calzone (i), folded & stuffed pizza
cameriera, waitress
cameriere, waiter

caffè.

camicia, in, poached
camomilla, camomile tea
camoscio, small deer (chamois)
campagnola, alla, w/vegetables & herbs
Campari, red aperitif w/a bitter, quinine taste
campo, del, wild. *Cicoria del campo* is wild chicory
candita (o), candied
canederli, dumplings made w/ham, sausage & breadcrumbs
canestrelli, sweet pastry/small sea snail or scallop
cannella, cinnamon
cannellini, small white beans found in Tuscany
cannelloni, large tube pasta stuffed w/fillings
cannelloni al forno, stuffed & browned in oven
cannelloni alla Barbaroux, stuffed w/ham, veal & cheese
cannelloni alla laziale, stuffed w/meat & onions
cannelloni alla napoletana, stuffed w/ham & cheese
   w/tomato & herb sauce
cannelloni alla piemontese, stuffed w/veal, ham & cheese
cannocchie, see *canoce*
cannoli alla siciliana, *ricotta* cheese-filled pastry
   w/sugar glaze
cannolicchio, razor-shell clam
cannolo (i), custard-filled pastry w/candied fruit or sweet
   white cheese (*ricotta*). This
   also refers to a short pasta tube
canoce, Venetian word for
   cannocchie which is neither a
   shrimp nor a lobster but something in between
cantarello, chanterelle mushroom

Cantarello.

cantucci, almond biscuits
capelli d'angelo, thin noodle soup ("angel hair")
capellini, long, thin, fine spaghetti
capelunghe, razor clams
cape sante, scallops in Venice
capitone, large eel
capocollo, smoked pork salami
caponata, cold dish of eggplant & vegetables.
Eggplant, celery & onions are fried separately &
cooked in a sweet & sour sauce of raisins, tomatoes,
pine nuts, sugar & vinegar
caponata di melanzane, eggplant & pepper stew
cappelle di funghi, mushroom caps
cappelletti, rings of pasta filled w/ground meat.
Some think they look like little caps
cappello da prete, a triangular
sausage ("priest's hat")
cappero (i), caper
cappesante, scallops (means
"sacred shells")
capponcello ruspante al forno,
roast farm-raised capon
cappone, capon
cappon magro, vegetables & fish stacked high on a plate
cappuccino, coffee w/steamed milk
capra, goat
caprese, *mozzarella* & tomatoes. **Pasta caprese** is pasta
w/tomatoes, *mozzarella* & basil. *Caprese* means
from the island of Capri
capretto, baby goat
capretto al forno, roasted kid stuffed w/herbs
capretto alla pasqualina, roasted baby goat (an Easter dish)
capricciosa (o), chef's special (means "caprice" or "whim")
caprino, mild goat's-milk cheese
caprino fresco, a fresh goat's-milk cheese
caprino romano, hard goat's-milk cheese
capriolo, small deer (roebuck)
caraffa, carafe
caramellate, caramelized
caramella (e), candy (not chocolate)
caramello, caramel
carbonade, beef cooked in wine & onions
carbonara, pasta w/bacon (or ham), cheese, olive oil & eggs

"Cappello da prete" means, priest's hat.

carbonata, grilled pork chop. Sometimes this
refers to beef stew in red wine

carciofi alla giudea, deep-fried artichokes
(prepared in the shape of a rose).
This term means "Jewish-style artichokes"

carciofi alla romana, artichokes stuffed w/garlic, parsley &
mint & cooked in olive oil & white wine

carciofi in pinzimonio, raw artichokes in an oil dressing

carciofini in umido, artichole hearts sautéed in garlic & tomatoes

carciofini sott'olio, artichokes in olive oil

carciofino (i), small artichoke

carciofo (i), artichoke. The bottoms of artichokes are the *fondi
di carciofi*

cardo (i), cardoon, a vegetable that looks like celery
but tastes like artichokes

carciofo.

carne, meat

carne a carrargiu, spit-roasted meat

carne cruda all`albese, slices of raw steak

carne di cervo, venison

carne macinata, ground meat

carne per arrosto in pentola, pot roast

carne tritata, ground meat

carone, large white beans

carota (e), carrot

carpa/carpione, carp

carpaccio, thinly sliced raw beef w/sauce. Named by the owner
of Harry's Bar in Venice after a famous Venetian painter

carpaccio di branzino, slices of raw sea bass w/a sauce

carpione, in, served cold w/vinegar sauce

carrargiu, spit-roasted

carré, sliced bread ("square")

carrè di..., roast loin of...

*"Carré" means
square.*

carrello, al, served from the food cart

carrettiera, tuna, garlic & pork sauce

carruba, carob

carta, menu

carta da musica, flat, crispy bread of Sardinia. See *pane carasau*

carteddate/cartellate, fried pastry dipped in honey

cartoccio, al, roasted (often in a paper bag, foil or other
covering). The covering is opened at the table

carvi (grani di), caraway (seeds)

casa, house. *Della casa* means "house specialty"

casalinga (o), homemade

cascà, the Sardinian version of couscous

casoncelli, pasta stuffed w/ground meat

cassata, ice cream (or sweet *ricotta* cheese) w/candied fruit

cassata alla siciliana, *ricotta* cheese-filled layered cake
w/sugar glaze

cassata gelata, various flavors of ice cream w/candied fruit

casserola/casseruola, casserole

cassoela/cassoeula, pork casserole

castagna (e), chestnut

castagnaccio, chestnut cake

castagnole, chestnut fritters

castellana, stuffed veal cutlet

Castelli Romani, white table wine
from the area southeast of Rome

castrato, mutton

Cavoletti.

catalogna, a type of salad green (like spinach, often cooked)

cauladda, Sardinian soup of cabbage, beans, sausage & meats

cavalla, mackerel. Also refers to a female horse

cavatappi, tubular pasta in the shape of a corkscrew

cavatelli/cavatieddi, homemade pasta

caviale, caviar

caviale del sud, "caviar of the south." Calabrian dish of dried
small fish preserved in oil & powdered w/*peperoncino*

cavoletti, Brussels sprouts

cavolfiore, cauliflower

cavolini di Bruxelles/cavoli di Brusselle, Brussels sprouts

cavolo (i), cabbage

cavolo broccoluto, broccoli

cavolo riccio, kale

cavolo rosso, red cabbage

cavolo verde, green cabbage

cazzoeula, pork casserole

cecatelli, homemade pasta

cece (i), chickpea/garbanzo

ceche, baby eels

*EELS BREED in
fresh water &
mature in the
sea.*

ceci alla Pisana, chickpea stew

cedrata/cedro, a large fruit that resembles a lemon.
The peel is used for flavoring

cee alla Pisana, baby-eel dish from Pisa

cefalo, grey mullet

cena, dinner

*cena —
chain-ah*

cenci, fried pastry

cenci ~ chenchi

Centerbe, green herb liqueur
cèpes, porcini mushroom
Cerasella, cherry liqueur
cereale, cereal
cerfoglio, chervil
cernia, grouper
Certosino, green or yellow herb liqueur. This is also the name for a soft & mild cheese
cervella, brains
cervo, venison
cestino di frutta, a basket of fruit
cetriolino (i), pickle
cetriolo (i), cucumber

cervella. No grazie!

cevapcici, grilled meatballs found near Italian/Slovenian border
champagne, champagne
charlotte, spongecake & whipped-cream dessert
Chianti, well-known medium-bodied red wine from Tuscany. ***Chianti Classico*** comes from the center of the Chianti region, is aged for at least one year & is more complex. ***Riserva*** denotes a *Chianti* aged for at least two years
chiare, egg whites
Chiaretto, young & popular rosé wine
chifferi, "c"-shaped tubular pasta
chiocciola (e), snail/sea shell-shaped pasta
chiocciolina, little snail
chiocciolini, spiral-shaped buns
chiodi di garofani, cloves
chiodino (i) a type of mushroom
chiodo di garofano, clove
ciabatta, large, coarse bread loaf
ciauscolo, soft, fatty pork sausage
cialda (e), waffle/wafer
cialledda, vegetable soup w/bread, olives, tomato, hard-boiled eggs & olive oil. A specialty in Basilicata
cialsons/chialzons, sweet & sour pasta
ciambella/chiambella/ciambelline, donut (not fried like North American donuts)
cibo, food
cibreo, chicken-liver dish
cicale di mare, type of shrimp (this crustacean is found off the coast of Italy. The name means "grasshopper")

cicchetti/cicheti, snacks served in Venice. Similar to *tapas*

cicina, mixture of small fried fish

cicoria, chicory/endive

ciliegia (e), cherry

cima, stuffed veal served cold

cima alla genovese, veal stuffed w/mushrooms & sausage

cimalino, *cima* served w/beans. ***Cimalino di manzo*** is stuffed breast of beef

cime di rape, turnip greens

cinese, Chinese

cinghiale, boar

Cinque Terre, a dry, light white wine from the spectacularly beautiful five towns on the western coast of Italy

cioccolata, chocolate

cioccolata calda, hot chocolate

cioccolato, chocolate (hot chocolate)

ciociara, a seasoned meat sauce

cioppino, fish stew (this word is usually used only in the United States)

cipolla (e), onion

cipollina (e), chive

cipolline novelle, green onions

cipollotti, spring onions

ciriola, small eel

ciuppin, thick fish (& vegetable) soup

civraxin, Sardinian large bread loaf

cocco/noce di cocco, coconut

cocktail di vongole, clam cocktail (clams, olive oil & lemon)

cocomero, watermelon

cocozelle, zucchini

coda, tail

Cocomero.

coda alla vaccinara, oxtail stew in a tomato & garlic sauce

coda di bue, oxtail

coda di rospo, monkfish

coglioni di mulo, finely ground pork sausage threaded with a wide strip of lard. The name means "mule's balls"

cognac, cognac

colazione (prima), breakfast

collo, neck

colomba, dove-shaped cake. ***Colombo*** means pigeon

colombacchi, wild pigeon

coltello, knife

composta, stewed fruit (compote)

composta cotta, mixed cold, cooked vegetables

con, with

conchiglie, shell-shaped pasta. *Conchigliette* is a small version used in soup

condimento (i), condiment

confetti, sugared almonds (used in weddings & special occasions)

confettura, jam

con ghiaccio, on the rocks

coniglio, rabbit

coniglio all'agro, rabbit stewed in red wine

coniglio all'Anconetana, a stuffed-rabbit dish

cono, cone (as in ice cream cone)

con seltz, w/soda

conserva, preserves/jam/jelly

conserva di frutta, preserves/jam/jelly

consommè, consomme (clear soup)

consommè madrilena, clear tomato soup

consommè reale, chicken consomme

Coniglio.
CO-NEE-LEO

contadina, alla, usually means served in a tomato & mushroom sauce (means "peasant woman")

conto, check/bill

contorno (i), side dish/garnish. This often refers to a vegetable side dish

contrafiletto/controfiletto, sirloin

copata, honey & nut wafer

coperto, cover charge

coppa, cup/goblet/small bowl. *Coppa* can also refer to smoked ham or smoked bacon

coppa di frutta, fruit cup/fruit cocktail

coppa di gamberetti, shrimp cocktail

coppa gelato, cup of ice cream/sundae

coratella di abbacchio, lamb heart, lung & liver dish

corda, lamb-tripe dish

cordulla, Sardinian dish made w/intestines

coregone, a type of salmon

coriandolo, coriander

cornetti, string beans

cornetto, croissant

corona, large white bean

'Cornetto' means trumpet.

corposo, full-bodied wine

corretto, coffee or *espresso* w/a shot of alcohol

Cortese, dry white wine

Corvo, dry, light white wine from Sicily

cosce di rana, frogs' legs

coscetta, leg/drumstick

coscia, leg

cosciette di rane, frogs' legs

cosciotto, leg

cosciotto di agnello, leg of lamb

cosciotto di porcello, leg of young lamb

costa, rib/scallop

costa di manzo, rib roast/T-bone steak

costa di sedano, celery stalk

costarelle di abbacchio a scottadito, grilled lamb cutlet

costarelli, spareribs/pork chops

costata, chop/beef steak. *Costata di vitello* is a veal chop. *Costata di manzo* is rib steak

costata alla fiorentina, grilled beef steak

costata alla pizzaiola, braised beef steak in a tomato sauce & *mozzarella* cheese

costate, rib steaks

costate d'agnello, rack of lamb

costatella, rib steak

costellata/costelleta/ costelletine, rib steak

costicini, pork spareribs

costine, pork spareribs

costola arrostita, rib roast

costolatura, beef loin

costole di manzo, prime rib

[handwritten margin note:] We have found that European cuts of meat often look nothing like cuts of the same name in the States.

costoletta (e), cutlet/chop (often coated in eggs & breadcrumbs & fried in butter)

costoletta alla bolognese, breaded veal cutlet w/tomato sauce, cheese & ham

costoletta alla milanese, breaded & fried veal cutlet

costoletta alla parmigiana, cutlet breaded & baked w/ *parmesan* cheese

costoletta alla siciliana, thin slices of veal or beef topped w/chopped garlic & *parmesan* cheese, breaded & deep-fried

costoletta alla valdostana, cutlet w/ham & cheese stuffing

costoletta alla viennese, wiener schnitzel
costoletta di vitello impanata, breaded veal cutlet
costolette di tonno, tuna steaks
costolette di vitello, veal chops
costolettine, lamb or pork chop
cotechino/coteghino, spicy pork sausage
cotognata, quince marmalade
cotogne, quince
cotoletta (e), cutlet, usually a veal cutlet
cotoletta alla bolognese, breaded veal cutlet topped w/ham,
   cheese & tomato sauce
cotto, cooked
cotto antico, bay leaf-flavored salami
cotto a puntino, medium done
courgette, zucchini
cozza (e), mussel

Courgette is actually a french word found on menus near the french border.

cozze alla marinara, mussels in white wine, garlic & parsley
cozze Posillipo, mussels in a spicy tomato sauce
crauti, sauerkraut
crema, cream/custard
crema caramella, custard w/caramelized-sugar topping
crema da montare, whipping cream
crema di, cream of
crema di funghi, cream of mushroom soup
crema di piselli, cream of pea soup
crema di pollo, cream of chicken soup
crema di verdura, puree of vegetables
crema fritta, fried-custard dessert
crema inglese, custard w/stewed fruit or cake
crème caramel, caramel custard
cremini, a type of mushroom
cremino, ice cream bar/a soft cheese
cren, horseradish
crescenza, a soft, buttery cheese (w/relatively low fat content)
crescionda, Umbrian dessert made from amaretto cookies,
   eggs, milk & unsweetened cocoa
crescione/crescione di fonte, watercress
crespelle, crêpes
crespelle alla fiorentina, spinach crêpes
crespolino, meat-filled pancake
croccheta (e), croquette
crocchette di patate, potato croquettes

crocchette di riso, deep-fried rice balls w/cheese in the center

crosta, crust (as in a pie crust)

crostaceo (i), shellfish

crostata, open-faced pie

crostata di frutta, fruit pie

crostini/crostoni, bread, fried or toasted in oil & topped
w/many ingredients/croutons

crostini alla napoletana, toast w/cheese & anchovies

crostini alla provatura, toasted diced bread
w/*provatura* cheese

crostini di mare, shellfish on fried bread

crostini di milza, toast w/veal paté

crostini Fiorentina, toast w/liver paté

crostini in brodo, croutons in broth

crostone di polenta, roasted meat (usually game) served on a
round base of *polenta*

crudo, raw

crusca, bran. This also refers to a bread found in Ticino w/thick
crust & dusted w/flour

cubbaita, nougat w/almonds, honey & sesame seeds

cucchiaio, spoon

cuccia, layered dish of slow-roasted meats, tomato sauce &
grains. A specialty in Calabria

cucina, cuisine

culaccio, rump meat

culatello, ham cured in white wine

cumino, cumin

cunillu, Sardinian word for rabbit

cuoco, chef

cuore (i), heart

cuore di sedano, celery heart

cuori di carciofi, artichoke hearts

curry, curry

cuscusu di Trapani, couscous

Cynar, after-dinner drink made of artichokes

daino, deer

da portar via, to go

datteri di mare, mussels

dattero (i), date

decaffeinato, decaffeinated

del giorno, of the day

della casa, of the house

"Cucina" means kitchen and cooking

"Decaffeinato" is becoming more common but be prepared for a condescending smile.

53

dente, al, pasta cooked until it's still slightly firm
   (means "to the tooth")

dentice, a Mediterranean fish (dentex) similar to sea bream

denti d'elefante, tubular pasta (like *macaroni*)
   (means "elephant's tooth")

di, of

diavola/diavolicchio, usually means served w/pepper or chili
   peppers. Can also mean a dish cooked over a flame since
   the terms mean "devil"

digestivo, after-dinner drink

diavolo-devi (handwritten)

disossata, boned rib steak

di stagione, in season

ditali, small tubular pasta for soup,
   often called thimbles. ***Ditalini*** is the
   smaller version of this pasta

diverso, varied

dolce (i), dessert/sweet/pastry. ***Dolce*** can also mean sweet win

Dolcetto, fruity, dry red wine from Piedmont

dolci di Taglierini, sweetened noodle (taglierini) cake

dolcificante, artificial sweetener

dorato (a), browned/golden brown

Doria, alla, w/cucumbers

e means and. (handwritten)

dragoncello, tarragon

é with an accen (handwritten)

e, and

eliche, spiral pasta.

means is. (handwritten)

   Often refered to as propellers

elicoidali, tubular pasta w/straight edges

emmenthal, Swiss cheese

empanata, breaded

entrecìte/entrecote di bue, boneless rib steak

erbazzone, vegetable pie

erbe, herbs

erbette, cooked greens

espresso, *espresso* (strong, small coffee)

espresso doppio, a double serving of *espresso*

espresso macchiato, *espresso* w/a small amount of foamy mil
   on top. Compare this to ***latte macchiato***

Est Est Est, a dry, semi-sweet white wine

Etna, red & white Sicilian wines

etto, fish dishes are frequently served by the *etto*
   (or 100 grams)

fagianella, bustard (bird)

fagiano, pheasant

fagioli al fiasco, slow-cooked Tuscan bean dish served
w/garlic, herbs & olive oil

fagioli alla maruzzara, beans in an oregano & tomato sauce

fagioli all'Uccelloto, white beans in a tomato sauce

fagioli bianchi, white beans

fagioli bianco di Spagna, lima beans

fagioli cannellini, small white beans

fagioli con le cotiche, beans in a tomato sauce w/slices of pork

fagioli cotti al forno, baked beans

fagioli freschi, fresh beans

fagioli lessati al forno, boiled baked beans

fagioli lessi, shelled, boiled beans

fagiolino (i) green bean/French bean

fagioli rampicanti, runner beans

fagioli rossi, red kidney beans

fagioli sgranati, fresh shelled beans

fagioli toscani, cooked white-bean dish

fagioli verdi, green beans

fagiolo (i), bean

fagottini, food wrapped around a filling

Falerno, dry white & red wines

fame, hungry

faraona, guinea fowl

farcito (a), stuffed

farfalle/farfallette, bow-tie or butterfly-shaped pasta

farfalline (i), bow-tie or butterfly-shaped pasta

farina, flour

farinata, baked pancake made from olive oil, chickpea flour,
salt & pepper (eaten as a snack)

farricello, barley

farro, red bean & barley porridge

farsumagru, veal or beef roll stuffed w/ham,
bacon, cheese, onions & parsley.
A Sardinian specialty

fasolini, scallops

fatto in casa, homemade

fava (e), broad bean. Sometimes called
fave grande or *fave España*

favarella, bean soup

favata, bean, sausage & bacon casserole

fave al Guanciale, broad beans cooked w/bacon & onions

fagioli.

farfalle.

farricello.

fave e cicoria, pureéd fava beans, sautéed chicory & olive oil. A specialty in Apulia

fegà, liver in Venice

fegatelli di maiale, pork liver

fegato (fegatini), liver.
Fegatini di maiale are pork livers;
fegatini di pollo are chicken livers

fegato alla veneziana, liver & onions

fegato di vitello, calf's liver

liver in Venice, liver in Milwaukee... No grazie

Fernet, a bitter digestive liqueur

ferri, ai, sliced & grilled (means "on iron")

fesa, leg of veal

fesa in gelatina, roast veal w/aspic jelly

fetta di/fette di, slice of...

fettina, small slice

fettuccine (i), long, flat, thin ribbon noodle

fettuccine Alfredo, thin ribbon noodles w/cream, butter & nutmeg

fettuccine alla Panna, thin ribbon noodles w/cream, butter & nutmeg

fettuccine in brodo, noodle soup

fettuna, toasted or grilled over an open fire w/garlic & olive oil

fettura di melacotogne, quince jam

fiamma, alla, flamed

fiammifero (i), match

fianco, flank

fiasco, straw-covered bottle

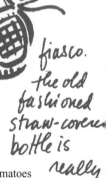

fiasco. the old fashioned straw-covered bottle is really a novelty now.

fichi d'India/fichi indiani, prickly pears

fichi in sciroppo, figs in syrup

fichi mandorlati, figs stuffed w/almonds

fico (fichi), fig

fidelanza, spaghetti in tomato sauce in Liguria

filetti (di pomodoro), a sauce of sliced tomatoes

filetto (i), fillet or tenderloin

filu e ferru, Sardinian *grappa*

finferlo, an orange-colored mushroom

finocchiata, pork cured w/fennel & pepper

finocchio, fennel (some think fennel has a licorice flavor)

finocchiona, fennel-flavored salami

fiocchetto, cold cut made from the leg of pork

fiocchi, flakes

fiocchi di granoturco, cornflakes

fiocco, ham shoulder

fior di latte, *mozzarella* made from cow's milk

fiore, flower

fiorentina, alla, w/oil, tomatoes & herbs
   (sometimes w/peas or spinach)

fiori con ripieno, stuffed zucchini flowers

fiori di zucca, zucchini flowers served either filled w/cheese,
   battered & fried or as a pizza topping

fiori di zucca fritti, fried zucchini flowers

flambé, flamed

focaccia, flat bread topped w/olive oil & sometimes cheese
   &/or onions. Can also mean cake

focaccia barese, stuffed pizza. A specialty of Apulia

focaccia di vitello, veal patty

foglia (e), leaf

foglia di alloro/foglia di lauro, bay leaf

foglia di vite, vine leaf

foiolo, tripe (stomach lining)

folpetto, the Venetian word for baby octopus

fondo di carciofo, artichoke heart

fonduta, melted cheese (fondue)

fontina, mild cheese (soft & creamy)

forchetta, fork

formaggini d'Alpe, cow's-milk cheese found in Ticino

formaggini di capra, fresh goat's-milk cheese found in Ticino

formaggio (formaggi), cheese

formaggio di fossa, aged sheep's-milk cheese
   from Le Marche

forno, al, baked

forte, strong

fracosta, rib steak

fragola (e), strawberry

fragole di bosco/fragoline di bosco, wild strawberries

fragolino, sea bream

fragolone, large strawberries

Frangelico, hazelnut-flavored cordial

frappé, milk shake

frascarelli, tiny *gnocchi*

Frascati, dry to slightly sweet white wine

frascota di bue, rib steak

frattaglie, giblets

freddo (i)/fredda (e), cold/iced. *Tè freddo* is iced tea
fregolotta, flour, cornmeal & almond cake
fregula, dumpling soup
Freisa, dry to slightly sweet red wine
fresca (o), fresh/not cooked
freschi, wild mushrooms
fresco, al, outside (in the fresh air)

Freschi –
FRESS - KEE

fricando, round of veal
fricassea, fricassee
fricò, cheese pancake
friggere, deep-fried (to deep fry)
frittata, omelette
frittata casalinga, plain omelette
frittata semplice, plain omelette
frittatina di patate, potato omelette
frittella (e), pancake/fritter
fritti ascolani, mixed fry of lamb chops, brains, olives
    & zucchini
fritto (a)/fritti (e), fried/deep-fried
fritto alla milanese, breaded & deep-fried
fritto alla napoletana, deep-fried fish, cheese & vegetables
fritto alla romana, deep-fried sweetbreads
fritto di verdura, fried vegetables
fritto misto, mixed deep-fried fish, meat or vegetables
fritto misto alla Fiorentina, meat & vegetable fritters
frittura, frying/fry
frittura del paese, mixed floured & fried seafood
frittura di pesce, mixed dish of fried small fish, squid &
    shrimp
frizzante, semi-sparkling wine
frolla, tender (meat)/flaky pastry

frizzante.

frollini, biscuits
frullato, milk shake
frullato di frutta, fruit milk shake
frumento, wheat
frumentone, corn
frutta, fruit
frutta candita, candied fruit
frutta cotta, stewed fruit
frutta fresca, fresh fruit
frutta secca, dried fruit
frutti di bosco, berries

frutti di mare, seafood/seafood salad
fundador, w/brandy
funghetti, small mushroom-shaped pasta for soup
funghetto, al, sliced mushrooms cooked in garlic,
    onions & herbs
funghi trifolati, mushrooms sauteed in butter & garlic
fungo (funghi), mushroom
fuoco dell'Etna, strong, red Sicilian liquor
fusi, leg. *Fusi di pollo* is a chicken leg
fusilli, spiral-shaped pasta.
    Fusilli corti are short & *fusilli lunghi* are long
fusto, shank
galatina (in gelatina), pressed meat in aspic
galantina tartufata, truffles in aspic jelly
galletta, cracker/cookie. Can also refer to a mushroom or grape
galletto, chicken (cock)
Galliano, herb liqueur (yellow in color)
gallina, chicken (hen)
gallinaccio, woodcock/chanterelle mushroom
gallina faraona, guinea fowl
gallinella, waterfowl
gallinella faraona, guinea fowl
gallo, John Dory fish in Sicily
    (a firm-textured, white-fleshed
    fish w/a mild, sweet flavor
    & low fat content)

galletto.

gallo cedrone, grouse (a game bird)
gamba, leg/drumstick/shank
gamba di vitello, veal shank
gamberelli, shrimp
gamberetta di rana, frogs' legs
gamberetto (i), shrimp
gambero (i), prawn/crayfish
gamberoni (gamberetti), large prawn
ganocchio, type of prawn
garetto, beef shank
garganelli, handmade pasta which is a square rolled into a tube
    (the dough is made from eggs, flour, grated *parmigiano*
    & nutmeg)
garofolato, beef stew
gaspaccio, gazpacho (the cold, tomato-based Spanish soup)
gasata/gassata, carbonated

Gattinara, full-bodied red wine

gelatina, jelly/gelatine

gelato (i), ice cream/iced dessert

gelato al tartufo, ice cream w/chocolate sauce

gemelli, pasta made of two strands twisted
around each other. The term means "twins"

genovese, alla, w/herbs
(especially basil), olive oil
& garlic/w/meat & onions

Genovese basil is considered the most fragrant.

germe di grano, wheat germ

germinus, almond-meringue cookies
from Sardinia

germogli, sprouts

gesuita, rib steak

ghiacciato, chilled/iced

ghiaccio, ice

ghianchetti, small anchovies

ghiotta, alla, grilled or roasted

ghiozzo, mackerel

gesuito means Jesuit presumably because the priests got the best meat.

giallo d'uova, egg yolk

gianchetti, small anchovies

gianduia, chocolate & hazelnut ice cream

gianduiotti, hazelnut-and-chocolate candies

giambonette(i)/giambonetto, boned chicken roll w/filling

giardiniera, small pieces of vegetables (a garnish)

gigantoni, large tubular pasta (means "giant")

gioddu, yogurt in Sardinia

giorno, del, of the day

gin, gin *Good Guess!*

ginepro, juniper berry

ginestrata, chicken & sweet wine soup (a sweet & sour soup)
A Tuscan specialty

girarrosto, spit-roasted

girasole, sunflower

girello, rump

glassate, glazed

girasole means turns to the sun.

gnoccata al pomodoro, tomato pizza

gnocchetti, small *gnocchi*

gnocchetti alla Sarda/gnocchetti sarda, small pasta
dumplings in various sauces. A specialty in Sardinia

gnocchi, flour or potato dumplings

gnocchi alla marchigiana, *gnocchi* w/chicken-giblet sauce

gnocchi alla piemontese, little balls of flour, egg & potato

gnocchi alla romana, semolina (flour) dumplings

gnocchi di patate, little balls of potato, flour & egg

gnocco fritto, deep-fried rolls of pasta

gnocco ingrassato, *focaccia* w/*prosciutto*

gnudi, means naked (w/out pasta). Stuffing
only, such as in ***ravioli gnudi***

gnudi... don't pronounce the G. NOO.DEE

gnumariddi, a sweetbread dish

gomiti, "c"-shaped tubular pasta

gomma da masticare, chewing gum

gorgonzola, creamy, blue cheese (best-known Italian blue)

goulasch, goulash

graffo (i), doughnut

Kinda cute, hey?

grana, mild, hard cheese (similar to *parmesan*)

granatina, steak tartare (raw ground beef). In most parts of
Italy this term means Italian ice or shaved ice

granceola, spider crab. A specialty of Venice

granchio (di mare), crab

granciporro (i), crab

grande, large

granello, seed

gran farro, grain & bean soup

grani di, seeds of...

granita, coffee or fruit syrup served over crushed ice
(a "snow cone"). Originally made from snow from Mt. Etna

grano, wheat/corn

grano duro, duram wheat

grano padano, buttery, hard, seasoned cheese
w/a grainy texture

grano saraceno, buckwheat

granoturco/granturco, corn on the cob

granseola, a crab found in Venice

grappa, liquor made from grape pressings.
It's extremely strong

Grappa is a popular digestivo which can taste like heaven... or hell.

grappolo, a bunch
(as in a bunch of grapes)

grassi vegetali, vegetable oil

grasso (a), oily/fatty/fat/grease

graticola, grilled/broiled

gratin/gratinate, oven-browned w/cheese

gratinada, baked dish topped
w/grated cheese & breadcrumbs

gratis, free

grattugiato, grated

gratuito (a), free

gremolata, minced anchovies, parsely & lemon (used as a garnish)

grenadine, veal chunks (used in casserole dishes)

gricia, alla, w/bacon, onion, cheese & chili pepper

griglia, alla, grilled (usually charcoal grilled)

grigliata mista, mixed grill of meats or fish

Grignolino, high-quality red wine

grissino (i), long, thin bread stick

grongo, Conger eel

groppo, rump (meat)

groviera/groviera svizzera, sharp
  cheese w/holes (like Swiss cheese)

guancia.

guancia, pig's cheek. *Al guanciale* means cooked w/bacon &
  onions. Also refers to the delicacy of pig's cheek

guardaroba, coat room

guarnite, alla, served w/a garnish

guazzetto, usually refers to a stew (meat or fish). In Sardinia,
  this dish almost always contains capers

gubana, sweet bread roll (dried fruit & nut strudel found in
  Friuli-Venezia Giulia)

gulyas, beef stew found in Friuli-Venezia Giulia

gusti, flavors

hasce di manzo, hamburger patty

igname, yam

impanato (a), covered in breadcrumbs

impazzata di cozze/impepata di cozze, mussels cooked in
  their own juice w/black pepper, oil, parsley & garlic

incapriata, purée of fava beans & chicory

incasciata, layered dough, meat sauce, hard-boiled eggs, cheese

incluso (a), included

Indiana, all', w/curry (Indian style)

indivia, endive/chicory

indivia Belga, Belgian endive

insaccati, salami

insalata, salad

insalata cotta...
Love it!

insalata all'americana, shrimp & mayonnaise salad

insalata caprese, tomatoes, basil & *mozzarella* salad.
  Originally a specialty on the island of Capri, but now
  found everywhere in Italy

insalata cotta, cold, cooked vegetable salad

insalata di campo, field lettuce
insalata di cesare, Caesar salad
insalata di crudita, mixed raw vegetable salad
insalata di frutti di mare, seafood salad
insalata di funghi, raw mushroom salad *← not a favorite*
insalata di mare, seafood salad
insalata di patate, potato salad
insalata di petti di pollo, chicken salad w/walnuts
insalata di tonno, tuna salad
insalata di verdura cotta, boiled vegetable salad
insalata mista, mixed salad
insalata riccia, curly endive
insalata russa, diced potato & vegetable salad w/mayonnaise
insalata siciliana, salad featuring fennel & black olives
insalata verde, green salad
integrale, whole wheat
involtini al sugo, rolled veal cutlets w/ham & cheese & topped
  w/tomato sauce
involtini di cavolfiori, cabbage leaves stuffed w/meat
involtini di pesce, thin fish slices stuffed w/*prosciutto* & herbs
involtini di salvia, a deep-fried sage-leaf anchovy roll
involtini di vitello, veal roll usually stuffed w/salami & cheese
involtino (i), stuffed roll
iota, hearty vegetable soup (white beans, cabbage & bacon fat).
  A specialty of Trieste
Ischia, red & white wines from Southern Italy
I.V.A., abbreviation for Value Added Tax (V.A.T.)
jota, thick bean & sauerkraut soup (see Iota)
julienne, small strips of vegetables
kirsch, al, w/a clear cherry brandy
knoedel/knödeln, dumplings found in the *Krapfen...*
  Trentino-Alto Adige region   *sounds good!*
krapfen, doughnuts (Austrian name)
laccetto, mackerel
lacerto, mackerel
Lacrima Christi, popular red,   *Lacrima Christi -*
  white & rosé wines   *tears of Christ*
Lago di Caldaro, light red wine
Lagrein Rosato, rosé wine
Lambrusco, well-known red wine (sweet)
lamelle di fegato, thin slices of liver sautéed in butter
lampasciuni, wild onions

lampone (i), raspberry

lampreda, lamprey

lanzado, mackerel

Lampreda. Non grazie!

lardarellatta alla fiamma, larded & cooked on a grill

lardo, bacon/salt pork/lard

lardone, salt pork

lardoons, cured & fried pork

lardoso, meat fat

lasagne, thin layers of dough & meat, tomatoes, cheese & sauce (baked in the oven)

lasagne al forno, large strips of pasta cooked in sauce

lasagne alla portoghese, baked custard caramel

lasagne alla vincisgrassi, baked *lasagne* w/meatballs

lasagne verdi, spinach *lasagne*

latte, milk

latte al cacao, chocolate milk

latte di mandorla, almond milk

latte intero, whole milk

latte macchiato, steamed milk w/a small amount of *espresso.* Compare this to ***espresso macchiato***

latte magro, skim milk

latterini, poached fish dish

latte scremato, skim milk

latticini, small *mozzarella* balls

lattonzolo, suckling pig

lattuga (e), lettuce

lattuga romana, romaine lettuce

lauro, bay leaf

lavarello, a type of salmon

laziale, alla, w/onions

lecca-lecca, sucker/lollypop

leccia, pompano

leggero, light or weak/light wine

legume (i), vegetable

lenticchia (e), lentil

lepre, rabbit/hare

lepre in salmì, marinated rabbit ("jugged rabbit")

leprotto, young rabbit

lessato (a), boiled

lesso, boiled. This can also refer to meat or fish stew

letterato, small tuna fish

lievito, yeast/baking powder

Latte. generally not drunk by the glass.

Vernazza is one of the Cinque Terre, five beautiful towns
perched on dramatic cliffs above the sea.

If you visit Milan, be sure to take a stroll through the Galleria Vittorio Emanuele, the famous glass-domed shopping center. It's home to the elegant Savini restaurant.

This food shop in Naples has everything from mustard (*senape*) to dried tomatoes (*pomodoro secchi*) to balsamic vinegar (*aceto balsamico*).

Night view of the Duomo in Florence, within walking distance of many fine restaurants.

Tomatoes, basil and *mozzarella* salad (*insalata caprese*) was originally a specialty on the beautiful island of Capri, but is now found on menus throughout Italy.

For the cost of a cup of coffee or a drink, you can linger at a café and watch the world pass you by for as long as you want. It's one of Italy's greatest bargains.

The magnificent Trevi Fountain in Rome. A coin thrown into the fountain will guarantee your return to the "Eternal City."

Either you've had too much wine, or that's the
Leaning Tower of Pisa.

Pasta comes in hundreds of shapes. From upper left to lower
right, here are just a few: bow ties or "butterflies" (*farfalle*),
spirals (*rotini*), and "little ears" (*orecchiette*).

Gorgonzola, *parmigiano*, and *pecorino* cheeses (*formaggi*), Parma ham (*prosciutto di Parma*), red wine (*vino rosso*), and bread (*pane*). No trip to Italy would be complete without sampling these national favorites.

Walk through these doors, and you'll sample some of Venice's best dishes, including delicious *fiori di zucca* (zucchini flowers filled with cheese, battered and then fried).

There's no more romantic place to eat and drink than along the Grand Canal in Venice. Sip a glass of *Prosecco* (sparkling white wine) and watch the gondoliers float by.

Italy is a boot-shaped peninsula extending into the Mediterranean Sea. You'll find an abundance of seafood on menus, like these delicious grilled shrimp (*gamberetti*).

Look at the size of those jugs! Wine being delivered
door-to-door (or rather, canal-to-canal) in Venice.

We can't include photos of Italian food without showing a
pizza. (Believe it or not, this one had peas on it.)
Buon appetito!

lievito di birra, brewer's yeast

limonata.

limonata, lemonade/lemon soda

limoncello, alcohol & lemon-zest drink

limone (i), lemon. *Al limone* means w/lemon juice

lingua, tongue. This can also refer to sole (seafood)

linguine, flat noodles

liquore (i), liqueur. *Liquore Strega* is a sweet herb liqueur

liquoroso, fortified dessert wine

liscia/lisce, refers to smooth pasta (w/out ridges)

liscio, straight. *Brodo liscio* is plain broth

lissa, pompano in Venice

lista, menu

lista dei vini, wine list

livornese, alla, usually beans in tomato sauce
w/celery & onions

locale, local

lodigiano, a type of *parmesan* cheese

Lombarda, alla, served fried in butter w/lemon juice & parsley

lombata, loin/leg. *Lombata di maiale* is a pork chop. *Lombata di vitello* is a grilled veal chop

lombata ai sassi, floured steak sautéed in butter w/sage & fried
potatoes

lombatine, tenderloin or cut of meat for filet mignon

lombello, loin/leg

lombo di manzo, beef loin/sirloin

lombo di vitello, veal sirloin

lonza, loin

lucanica, spicy sausage

lucerna (e), grouper

luccio, pike

Lumaca.

lucullo, alla, raw beef (steak tartare)

Lugana, dry white wine

luganega, pork sausage. This spicy sausage from Basilicata
has many similar spellings such as *luganica* & *lucanica*

lumaca (lumache), snail. *Lumache* also refers to snail-shaped
pasta. *Lumachine* is a small version of this pasta
used in soup

lumache alla Bourguignonne, snails w/garlic butter
("Burgundy snails")

lunga, long (as in long pasta or *pasta lunga*)

lungo, lighter *espresso*

lupo di mare, sea perch

luvasu, sea bream

maccarello, mackerel

maccarones con bottarga, Sardinian pasta w/fish eggs

maccaruni di casa, Sicilian pasta dish served
  w/tomato & meat sauce

maccheroni, *macaroni*

maccheroni al pettine, pasta w/ridges usually served w/ragù

macchiato, coffee or *espresso* w/milk

macco di fave, broad bean, onion & tomato soup

macedonia di frutta, fruit salad

macedonia di legumi, mixed cooked vegetables

macinata, ground. *La carne macinata* is ground beef

madera, al, cooked in Madeira wine

mafaldine, pasta ribbons

maggiorana, marjoram

magro, dish w/no meat/lean.
  Ravioli di magro is stuffed pasta
  w/herbs & *ricotta* cheese

marjoram is a member of the oregano family.

maiale, pork

maionese, mayonnaise

mais, corn

malfatti di ricotta, *ricotta gnocchi. Malfatti* means badly
  made, a reference to the handmade dumplings in this dish

malloreddus, flavored dumplings found in Sardinia

malloreddus all'oristanese, saffron-flavored dumplings w/a
  sauce of Swiss chard, cream & eggs

maltagliata, *macaroni*

Mammole.

mammole, artichokes

mancia, tip

mandarino (i), tangerine/mandarin

mandorla (e)/mandorlata, almond

manicotti, stuffed (w/cheese & meats), baked pasta dish

mantecato, whipped ice cream. This also refers to a way to
  prepare cod

manzo (di bue), beef

manzo arrosto ripieno, stuffed roast

manzo lesso, boiled beef

manzo salato, corned beef

manzo stufato al vino rosso, beef stewed in red wine

maraschino/marasco, w/Maraschino (cherry-flavored liqueur

marchigiana, alla, a dish in the style of Le Marche (one of th
  regions of Italy), usually cooked w/chicken giblet sauce

mare, di, of the sea

mare-monti, a dish served w/mushrooms & shrimp

margarina, margarine

margherita, this term is used to describe a pizza w/tomato,
mozzarella & basil

marinara, alla, usually, but not always, means in tomato sauce
(usually w/garlic & onions). The term means "of the sea" or
"sailor's style," so can also refer to a dish w/seafood

marinata (o), marinated

maritozzo, soft bread roll

marmellata, marmalade/jam

marmellata d'arance, marmalade

marrone (i), chestnut. *Marrons glaces* are candied chestnuts

Marsala, fortified dessert wine from Sicily

marsala, al, in a Marsala (fortified dessert wine) sauce

Martini, vermouth

mascarpone, a soft, very creamy, fresh cheese (even for
cheese, it's high fat)

masenette, tiny crabs eaten whole (w/the shell)/Venetian word
for small soft-shelled crabs

matriciana, bacon, tomato & spices sauce

mattone, al, pounded flat (usually chicken) & roasted in a
brick oven

mazza da tamburo, a parasol-shaped mushroom

mazzancelle/mazzancolle, very large prawns

mazzancougni, very large prawns

medaglione, medallions

medallione, a grilled ham & cheese sandwich

media, medium

mela (e), apple

melacotogna, quince

melagrana, pomegranate

melanzana (e), eggplant

eggplant is a member of the same family as tomatoes, potatoes & peppers.

melanzane al funghetto, sautéed eggplant

melanzane alla Napoletana, eggplant Neopolitan style
(layered w/cheese & tomato puree & baked in an oven)

melanzane alla parmigiana, eggplant *parmesan* (w/tomatoes
& *parmesan* cheese)

melanzane ripiene, stuffed eggplant

melassa, molasses

meliga, cornmeal

melone, melon/canteloupe

menta, mint
mentine, mints
menù, menu
menù a prezzo fisso, set menu
menù turistico, fixed-price menu
merca, roast fish dish from Sardinia
merenda, late morning/afternoon snack
meringa, meringue
meringa chantilly, meringue shells filled w/whipped cream
meringato/meringhe/meringua, meringue
merlango, hake/cod/whiting
merlano, whiting, cod or hake
merluzzo, cod
messicani, veal scallops dish/veal rolls
mesticanza, mixture of salad greens
metà, half
mezzo (a), half
mezzelune ai pinoli, pine-nut cookies from Umbria
mezze maniche, short tubular pasta
miascia, bread & fruit pudding
midollo, marrow
miele, honey   *millefoglie means*
miglio, millet   *a thousand leaves*
milanese, alla, battered w/eggs & breadcrumbs & fried
Millefiori, herb-based liqueur
millefoglie, puff pastry/napoleon
millerighe, ridged tubular pasta (means "thousand lines"
   after the ridges in the pasta)
mimosa, spongecake & whipped-cream dessert
minerale, mineral (as in *acqua minerale* or mineral water)
minestra (minestre), soup (usually thick soup)
minestra al farro, soup made from the grain
   emmer (a hard red wheat)
minestra di cipolle, onion soup
minestra di fagioli, bean soup
minestra di farina tostata, toasted-flour soup
minestra di farro, "spelt" soup. Wheat (spelt) soup w/ ham bo
minestra di funghi, cream of mushroom soup
minestra di lenticchie, lentil soup
minestra di pomodoro, tomato soup
minestra di riso, rice soup
minestra in brodo, broth w/noodles or rice & chicken livers

minestra maritata, meat broth & vegetable soup

minestre di piscialetto, dandelion-greens soup

minestrina, soup (usually clear)

minestrone, bean & vegetable soup w/noodles, vegetables, rice

minestrone alla genovese, vegetable soup
w/*macaroni* & spinach

minestrone verde, thick vegetable soup w/herbs & beans

mirabella (e), small plum

mirtillo (i), blueberry. The word *mirtilli* is also used for berries
in general & for cranberries

mischianza, salad of wild greens, herbs & edible flowers

misoltini, salted & dried shad (fish)

misticanza, salad of wild greens, herbs & edible flowers

misto/misti, mixed

misto del golfo/misto del paese, mixed floured & fried seafood

misto mare, mixed floured & fried seafood

mitilo, mussel

moka, mocha

molto, very

montanara, alla, has many meanings but generally means
w/red wine sauce or w/vegetables

montare, to whip (usually refers to cream)

montebianco/Mont Blanc, pyramid of sweetened chestnuts &
whipped cream (named after Mont Blanc) *Mont Blanc
is the
French side of
Monte Bianco
mountain.*

Montepulciano, full-bodied, dry red wine

montone, mutton

monzittas, snails in Sardinia

mora (e), blackberry

mormora, small fish found in the Mediterranean

mortadella, luncheon meat w/pistachio nuts & peppercorns

morto, pot roast

mosca, con la, a drink (usually *Sambuca*) served "w/the
fly"(*con la mosca*). The "fly" is a coffee bean in the glass

moscardino (i), small squid

Moscatello/Moscato, muscatel (table & dessert white & red
wines from the muscat grape)

mostarda, mustard. This word is rarely used. Most use *senape*

mostarda di frutta, candied fruits in syrup/preserved fruits in
a mustard sauce/fruit chutney

mousse al cioccolato, chocolate mousse

mozzarella, a soft, fresh (unripened), slightly sweet cheese

mozzarella di bufala, *mozzarella* made from buffalo milk

mozzarella in carrozza, fried *mozzarella* sandwich
   (means "in a carriage")
muddica, breadcrumbs in Sicily
muggine, grey mullet
muscoletti, shank
muscoli, mussels. This word is rarely used. Most use *cozze*
muscoli alla marinara, steamed mussels dish
musetto, salami
napoletana, ("Naples-style") w/tomato sauce (w/out meat)
nasello, whiting/hake/cod
naturale, plain/natural
nave, di, w/seafood
navone (i), turnip
`nduja, Calabrian pork sausage
Nebbiolo, full-bodied dry red wine
nepitella, an herb similar to mint
nero (a), black
nervetti, calf's foot dish (tendons of calves' feet).
   A Venetian specialty
nespola, medlar (a tart fruit)
nidi di rondine, pasta rolls
nocciola (e), hazelnut
noccioline americane, peanuts
nocciole, nuts
noce (i), nut/walnut. Can also refer to the top round of veal
noce di cocco, coconut
nocelli, walnut-raisin cookies
noce moscata, nutmeg
nocepesca, nectarine
noci d'anacardo, cashews
Nocillo/Nocino, liquor made from walnuts
nodino (i), chop/small grilled pork chop
non, not
non fumatori, no smoking
non gassata, still or not carbonated
nonna, alla, this can be any sauce served w/pasta. The term
   means "grandmother" & there are as many variations of
   "alla nonna" as there are grandmothers
norcina, sausage & cheese sauce. After the town of Norcia
Norma, alla, this usually refers to a dish served w/eggplants,
   tomatoes, basil & sometimes *ricotta* cheese
nostrale/nostrano, home-grown/local

Navone .

nervetti...
I don't
think so.

novellame, a spread of salted anchovies & *peperoncino* sauce
novello/novelli, fresh/tender
o, or
oca, goose
occhiate, orata (a fish)
occhi di lupo, small tubular pasta
   "wolves' eyes")
olio, oil/olive oil
olio d'arachide, peanut oil
olio da tavola, salad oil
olio di cartamo, safflower oil
olio di girasole, sunflower oil
olio di grano/olio di granturco, corn oil
olio di palma, palm oil
olio di semi, seed oil/corn oil
olio d'oliva, olive oil
olio santo, chili-infused oil
oliva (e), olive (*nere*, black, *verdi,* green)
olive agrodolci, olives in sugar & vinegar
olive ascolane, large green olives. *Olive all'ascolana*,
   in Le Marche, olives are stuffed meat & fried in olive oil
ombra, glass of wine in Venice. This word is usually used at a
   bar & not at a restaurant
ombrina, umbrine (seafood/bass)
omelette, omelette
omelette casalinga, plain omelette
omelette semplice, plain omelette
oranciata, orangeade
orata, a fish found in the Mediterranean (porgy)
oratino, a small *orata* fish
orecchiette, small ear-shaped pasta
orecchiette con le cime di rapa, small ear-shaped pasta
   w/turnips. A specialty in Apulia
origano, oregano
ortaggi, vegetables/greens/herbs
Orvieto, light, dry, white wine from Orvieto in Umbria
orzata, almond or barley-flavored water
orzetto, barley & potato soup
orzo (i), rice-shaped pasta. Can also refer to barley
osso, bone
ossobuco (ossibuchi), braised veal-shank dish. You may be
   given a marrow spoon to eat the marrow in the bone

*Olio d'oliva
we never leave
Italy without
a bottle*

ossobuco alla milanese, veal shank, tomatoes, garlic & wine

ostrica (ostriche), oyster

ovalina, a type of *mozzarella* cheese

ovolo (i), a rare (& delicious) mushroom w/an orange & scarlet color. Sometimes called Caesar's mushroom

pacchetto, package

paciugo, parfait

padella, in, fried

paesana, alla, usually means served w/bacon (or sausage), potatoes, carrots & other vegetables

paeta, spit-roasted turkey

pagaro/pagello, sea bream/porgy

paglia e fieno, pasta dish w/yellow (egg) & green (spinach) pasta (means "straw & hay")

pagliarino, soft, mild cheese

pagliata, a dish containing organ meat

pagnotta, loaf

pagnotta del cacciatore, game birds roasted in dough

pagro, sea bream/porgy

paiata, spit-roasted turkey

paillard, beef rib steak or veal cutlet pounded thin & grilled

pajata, a dish containing organ meat

palamito, bonito fish

palemone, prawns

pallina, scoop (as in scoop of ice cream). The word really means "marble"

palomba/palombaccia, pigeon

palombacci, an Umbrian dish of small birds cooked whole on a spit

palombo, dogfish/shark found in Sicily

palomba.

panafittas, dried bread broken into pieces & boiled (like pasta), then served in a tomato sauce in Sardinia

They're all over the down place.

panardo, a thirty-course feast served in Abruzzo

panata, bread soup

pancetta, bacon (cured pork belly)

pancetta arrotolata, rolled bacon flavored w/cloves

pan có Santi, sweet bread w/raisins, dates, honey & walnuts. "Saints' bread" is eaten around All Saints Day (November 1

pan di Genova, almond cake

pan di Spagna, spongecake

pandolce, cake w/dried fruit

pandoro (di Verona), star-shaped light cake w/sugar topping

pane, bread/loaf

pane bianco, white bread

pane bigio, whole-wheat bread

pane carasau, flat crispy bread found in Sardinia. Also known
as *carta da musica* (music paper)

pane di segale, rye bread

pane e coperto, the charge for bread & for sitting at the table

pane frattau, *pane carasau* topped w/tomato sauce, grated
cheese & a fried egg. A specialty in Sardinia

pane grattugiato, breadcrumbs

pane integrale, whole-wheat bread

panelle, chickpea fritters

pane nero, dark bread

pane pepato, gingerbread

pane piccante, gingerbread

pane scuro, pumpernickel bread

pane toscano, sourdough bread

pane tostato, toast

panettone, spiced cakes or
coffeecakes w/candied fruits

panforte, flat, hard fruitcake

pan grattato, breadcrumbs

*Pane.
the Italians,
like the French,
are fiercely
proud of their
bread.*

panicielli d'uva passula, grapes wrapped in leaves & baked

panino (i), roll/sandwich

panino imbottito, sandwich

paniscia, rice, sausage & bean soup

pan matteloch, honey bread found in the lake country

pan meino, cornmeal bread/cake (millet bread) w/elderflowers

panna, cream

panna, alla, served in a cream sauce or w/creamy gravy

panna, con, in a cream sauce/w/cream

panna cotta, rich cream custard

panna da montare/panna montata, whipped cream

pannocchia, corn on the cob

panpepato, gingerbread or hazelnut cake

pansoti/pansotti, triangular-shaped filled pasta

pan tostato, toast

panzanella, bread & vegetable salad

panzerotti, baked (or deep-fried) dough filled w/pork, cheese, tomatoes or other ingredients

panzoni, stuffed ravioli dish

paparot, cornmeal & spinach dish from Friuli-Venezia Giulia

pappa al pomodoro, tomato & bread soup

pappardelle, long, flat, wide pasta

pappardelle al sugo di lepre/pappardelle alla lepre, strips of pasta w/rabbit sauce

paprica, paprika

pardulas, Sardinian pastries filled w/cream cheese

parigina, hamburger buns. In Sicily, this refers to bread

parmigiana, alla, w/*parmesan* cheese & tomatoes

parmigiana di melanzane, baked slices of eggplant layered w/*parmesan* cheese, tomatoes & *mozzarella*

parmigiano, *parmesan* cheese usually served grated

parmigiano-reggiano, the "real" name for *parmesan* cheese

partenopea, means "Naples' style," the same as *Napolitana*

Pasqualina, "Easter style" which can mean roasted in an oven w/olive oil, onion, garlic, black olives & celery. *Torta Pasqualina* is a pie featuring artichokes

passate di legumi, puree of vegetables

passatelli, pasta of *parmesan* cheese, eggs & breadcrumbs

passato, puree

passato di verdura, cream of vegetable soup

passera di mare, flounder

passera pianuzza, flounder

passerino, flounder

pasta, pasta (dough made of flour, oil, butter, eggs & water). The first course in Italy. If you find *-ette* or *-ini* after pasta, this means a smaller version of pasta. For example, *pennette* & *pennini* are smaller versions of *penne*. If you find *-oni* after pasta, this means a large pasta like *rigatoni*. *Pasta* that starts w/*taglia* is made of long, thin strips. *Pasta* can also mean pastry

pasta al forno, any pasta mixed w/a sauce & baked

pasta alla Norma, pasta w/tomatoes, basil & eggplant topped w/*ricotta* cheese

pasta asciutta, any pasta not eaten in soup

pasta con le sarde, pasta w/fresh sardines

pasta d'arachide, peanut butter

pasta di olive, olive paste

pasta e ceci, pasta & chickpea soup

pasta e fagioli, pasta & bean soup

pasta frolla, puff pastry

pasta in brodo, pasta in broth

pasta 'ncasciata, pasta baked w/eggplant, salami, tomato/basil

pasta reale (paste reali), marzipan cake (means "royal pastry")

pasta sfoglia, puff-pastry dough

paste, pastries

pastella, batter for frying

pasticceria (e), pastry

pasticcetti, small tarts

pasticciata, baked pasta (in a casserole)

pasticcini da te, teacakes/small pastries

pasticcino (i), cake/small pastry/tart

pasticcio, pastry/pie. Also the Venetian word for baked lasagne

pasticcio di maccheroni, sweet pie containing meat sauce

pastiera napoletana, *ricotta* cheese-filled pastry

pastina, small pasta usually used in soup

pastina in brodo, pasta served in soup

pastissa, pot pie

pasto, meal

patata (e), potato

patate al lesso, boiled potatoes

patate al ghiotto/patate alla ghiottona, stuffed baked potatoes

patate americane, sweet potato

patate arroste, roasted potatoes

patate bollite, boiled potatoes

patate dolci, sweet potato

patate fritte, fried potatoes/french fries

patate in padella, potatoes fried in a pan

patate lesse, boiled potatoes

patate novelle, new potatoes

patate rosolate, roasted potatoes

patate saltate, potatoes sliced & sautéed

patate tenere, new potatoes

patatine fritte, french fries/chips

patatine novelle, small roasted potatoes

pate/paterini, pâté

pecora, sheep/ewe

pecorino, hard, sharp cheese usually served grated.
Pecorino alla griglia is a Sardinian specialty of grilled
pecorino cheese

pellegrine, scallops

[handwritten margin note:] Anti – before / pasto – meal / antipasto.

75

penne, tube-shaped pasta (cut at an angle)

pennette, smaller version of *penne*

penneziti, larger version of *penne*

pennoni, the largest version of *penne*

peoci, mussels. Also the Venetian word for "head lice"

pepata di cozze, mussels in a black pepper, oil & garlic sauce

pepato, peppered

pepe, black pepper

pepe di Giamaica, allspice

peperonata, tomatoes, peppers & onion stewed together

peperoncino (i), small, spicy pickled pepper

peperone (i), pepper

peperoni alla brace, roasted marinated peppers

peperoni imbottiti, stuffed peppers

peperoni ripieni, stuffed peppers

peperoni rossi, red peppers

peperoni sott'aceto, pickled chilis

peperoni verdi, green peppers

pera (e), pear

perciatelli, hollow spaghetti noodles

per contorno, meal includes salad or side dish

pere helene/pere elena, poached pear served in vanilla ice cream & topped w/chocolate sauce

pernice, partridge

persico, perch

pesca (pesche), peach

pesca melba, peaches in syrup w/ice cream & whipped cream

pescatora/pescatore, seafood sauce for pasta & rice dishes

pescatrice, angler fish

pesce, fish

pesce carpionata, marinated fish in herbs

pesce in saor, fish in a sauce of onion, raisin, pine nut & vinegar. A specialty in Veneto

pesce persico, perch

pesce San Pietro, John Dory fish (a firm-textured, white-fleshed fish w/a mild, sweet flavor and low fat content)

pesce sciabola, an eel-like fish

pesce serra, bluefish

pesce spada, swordfish

pesce stocco, cod

pesce turchino, mackerel

pesche, peaches

pesche aurora, spongecake soaked in peach liqueur

pesto, basil, oil, garlic & pine-nut sauce

petonchio, scallops

petroniana, alla, can mean many things, most frequently breaded & fried & topped w/melted cheese

pettine (i), small scallop

petto, breast (of poultry)

petto alla principessa, chicken floured & fried in butter & served w/an egg on top

petto all'arancio, chicken in an orange sauce

petto di pollo, chicken breast

peverada, chicken liver & anchovy sauce *only for the brave.*

pezzenta, pork salami

pezzo, piece

piacere, of your own choice (your pleasure)

piadina, soft, flat bread

pianuzza, flounder/halibut

piastra, grilled on a flat steel plate

piattino, saucer

piatto (i), dish/plate. *Piatti freddi* means cold dishes

piatto del giorno, dish of the day

piccante, highly seasoned (hot)

piccata (e), veal scallop

piccata all'allegro, veal scallop fried in butter w/lemon juice

piccata alla Lombarda, veal scallop fried in butter w/lemon juice & parsley

piccata di vitello, veal cooked in lemon & parsley

piccatina, veal scallop dish

piccioncino, young pigeon

piccione, pigeon

piccione selvatico, wild pigeon

piccolo (i)/piccola (e), small

pici, eggless pasta

piede (i), foot

piemontese, sauce w/truffles ("Piedmont style")

pietanza, dish/main course

pignata, lamb or goat w/herbs. A specialty from Basilicata named after the terra-cotta pot it's cooked in

pimento, pimento/allspice

pimiento, sweet red peppers

pinoccate/pinocchiata, almond & pine-nut cake

pinolata, pine-nut dessert cake found in Tuscany

pinolo (i), pine nut

Pinot Grigio, light, fruity white wine

pinsimonio/pinzimonio, oil, pepper & salt dressing/oil & mustard dressing for dipping

pinza, yellow flour, pine nut & raisin cake from Veneto

pipe, pasta similar to *lumache* (a snail-shaped pasta)

pisello (i), pea

pistacchi, pistachio nuts

pitta, pizza either stuffed or topped with many ingredients. Popular in Calabria

piviere, plover (bird)

pizza, pizza

pizza alla marinara, the "true" pizza: tomato, olive oil & oregano

Pizza... Man's highest culinary achievement.

pizza alla napoletana, pizza w/cheese, capers, tomatoes, anchovies, olives & *mozzarella*

pizza alla siciliana, pizza w/salami or ham, anchovies, olives, tomatoes & *mozzarella*

pizza bianca, pizza bread topped w/sea salt & olive oil

pizza capricciosa, same as *pizza quattro stagioni*

pizza di Pasqua, cheese bread

pizzaiola, w/tomato & garlic sauce

pizzaiolo, pizza man (the maker of pizzas)

pizza margherita, pizza w/tomato, basil & *mozzarella*

pizza marinara, pizza w/garlic, oil & oregano. Can also refer to a pizza w/black olives, anchovies, tomatoes & capers

pizza quattro stagioni, w/seafood, cheese, artichokes & ham in four sections. Means "four seasons" & is a pizza which has a different topping for each quarter

pizza rustica, common in central Italy; serves large rectangular pizzas with thicker crusts and more toppings than usually found in a *pizzeria*. You can order as much as you want, and pay by weight

pizzelle, small (fried) pizzas

pizzetta, small pizza

pizzoccheri, pasta made w/buckwheat flour

polenta, cornmeal mush

polenta concia, *polenta* w/cheese

polenta di grano saraceno, buckwheat *polenta*

polenta dolce, sweet *polenta* dessert

polenta e osei, *polenta* w/roast fowl

polenta grassa, butter, fontina cheese & *polenta*

polenta pasticciata, *polenta* served w/meat sauce, cheese, mushrooms & sauce (*polenta* pie)

polipetto (i), small squid/baby octopus

polipo (i)/polpo (i), octopus

pollame, poultry

pollastra/pollastrello, young chicken

pollo al mattone/pollastrino al mattone, chicken pounded flat & roasted in a brick oven

pollo al mattone is a favorite!

polletto, spring chicken

pollo, chicken

pollo alla diavola, highly spiced, grilled chicken

pollo alla Marengo, sautéed chicken dish with many ingredients (usually tomatoes, mushrooms & onions). The dish takes its name from the town of Marengo, where Napoleon defeated the Austrians

pollo alla romana, fried chicken pieces, bacon & garlic

pollo all'arrabbiata, "Enraged chicken" (a spicy chicken dish)

pollo arrosto, roasted chicken

pollo fritto Fiorentina, chicken marinated in oil, lemon juice & herbs

pollo in bellavista, roasted chicken dish w/vegetables

pollo novello, spring chicken

pollo piccata al Marsala, chicken pounded thin & fried in butter & Marsala wine

pollo scarpariello, boneless chicken w/lemon, garlic & parsley

polpa, lean meat/flesh

polpetielle, baby octopus

polpetta (e) di carne, meatball

polpetti affogati, small octopuses cooked w/tomatoes (means "drowned octopuses")

polpettine (i), meatball. *Polpettine di pesce* is a seafood ball

polpettone, meat loaf

polpi arricciati, "curled octopus." An octopus dish in which the octopus is curled by beating & twirling it in a basket

polpo, octopus

polpo in purgatorio, octopus sautéed in oil w/tomatoes & peppers

pomi d'oro, the original name for tomato (means "golden apple"). It's believed that the tomato arrived in Europe w/a golden color that turned red under the hot Mediterranean sun

pommarola (salsa di), tomato sauce

pomo (i), apple

pomodoro (i), tomato

pomodoro, al, w/tomato sauce

pomodoro doppio (concentrato), thick tomato paste

pomodoro pelati, peeled tomatoes in their own juice

pomodoro pumate, sun-dried tomato

pomodoro super cirio, thick tomato pureé

pomodori con tonno, tomatoes stuffed w/tuna

pomodori secchi, sun-dried tomatoes

pompelmo, grapefruit

popone, melon

porcecellino, suckling pig

porceddu/porcheddu, Sardinian word for roast suckling pig

porcello, young pig

porchetta, roast suckling pig stuffed w/herbs

porcini, mushrooms (the wild mushroom boletus)

porco, pork

porri dorati, battered & deep-fried leeks

porro (i), leek

portacenere, ashtray

portafoglio, veal cutlet stuffed
    w/herbs, cheese & other ingredients.
    This is also the word for wallet

porta cenere Can't get away from it in Italy.

portata (e), course

porto, port

portoghese, usually means
    w/tomato sauce

porzione, portion

posillipo, seafood sauce

praio, dorade (fish)/gilt-head bream

pranzo, lunch/dinner

presnitz, dessert made w/dried fruit from
    Fruili-Venezia Giulia

prezzemolo (i), parsley

prezzo, price

prezzo fisso, fixed price

prima colazione, breakfast

primavera, spring vegetables & cream sauce

primizie, spring vegetables or fruit

primo, first (as in *primo piatto,* first course)

principale, main (as in *piatto principale,* main course)

profiterole, filled ice-cream puff topped w/chocolate sauce &
   whipped cream
prosciutto, aged & cured ham
prosciutto affumicato, cured, smoked ham
prosciutto cotto, cooked or boiled ham
prosciutto crudo, salted, cured ham/Parma ham
prosciutto di cinghiale, smoked wild boar
prosciutto di San Daniele, a cured ham
   named after a town in the Friuli-Venezia Giulia region
prosciutto e melone, ham & melon
prosciutto di Parma, Parma ham
   (famous cured ham of Parma)
Prosecco, sparkling white wine from Veneto
provatura, soft, mild & sweet cheese
provenzale, onions, black olives, tomato & mushroom sauce
provolone, mild buffalo cheese
provolone dolce, mild, white, medium-hard cheese
provolone piccante, sharp cheese
prugna (e), plum
prugna secca (prugne secche), prune
pumaruolo/pumaruoro, tomato in Sicily & Campania
pumate, sun-dried tomatoes
punta di vitello, veal brisket
puntarelle, a salad green
punte di asparagi, asparagus tips
Punt e Mes, orange-flavored vermouth
   (drunk before meals)
puntino, a, medium done
punto, breast. *Punto* also means medium rare
purea, pureed/mashed
purea di fave, a puree of broad beans
   often spread on bread
purè di patate, mashed potatoes
puttanaio, a stew-like ratatouille
   (means "prostitute stew")

*Absdulti
favourite
2* (handwritten annotation)

puttanesca, tomato, black olives, capers & garlic sauce (the
   term means "prostitute"). Allegedly named because
   prostitutes could prepare this quick meal between
   "customers"
quadrello, pork loin
quadrello d'agnello, rack of lamb
quadretti, refers to small squares of pasta

quadrucci, square-shaped pasta for soup

quaglia (e), quail

quattro formaggi, four cheeses

quattro spezie, four spices combined
(pepper, cloves, juniper & nutmeg)

quattro stagioni, pizza
w/seafood, cheese,
artichokes & ham
in four sections

*Quattro Stagione
means
Four Seasons*

rabarbaro, rhubarb. This can also refer to an
after-dinner liqueur

radiatori, pasta shaped like a radiator

radicchio, red endive/red chicory (bitter red lettuce)

rafano, horseradish

ragnetto, rolls

ragno, sea bass

ragno di mare, spider crab

ragù, tomato-based meat sauce

ragusano, hard, slightly sweet cheese

ramolaccio, horseradish

Rana.

ranapescatrice, angler fish

rane, frogs or frogs' legs

rannocchi, frog or frogs' legs

rapa (e), turnip

rape rosse, beet root

raspante, farm-raised (usually chicken). Means "scratching"

Ratafia, black-cherry liqueur

rattatuia, ratatouille

ravanada, horseradish sauce

ravanello (i), radish

raviggiolo, goat's-milk cheese

ravioli, squares of pasta w/stuffing. *Raviolini* are half-circle
stuffed pasta

ravioli gnudi, ravioli stuffing (without the pasta)

ravioli verdi, spinach ravioli

razza, ray

recchie/recchietelle, the word in Apulia for *orecchiette* (ear-
shaped pasta)

remolazzitt, radish

rene (i), kidney

ribes, currants

ribes neri, black currants

ribes rossi, red currants

ribollita, vegetable soup (which means "reboiled") thickened
w/bread. There are many versions of this Tuscan soup

ricciarelli, marzipan &/or almond biscuits

riccio (di mare)/ricci (di mare), sea urchin

ricciola, amberjack (fish)

riccioli, small, curly pasta

riccolo, curly endive

Ribollita means Reboiled. (handwritten)

ricotta, similar to cottage cheese, sweetened when
used in desserts

ricotta al maraschino, *ricotta* cheese w/maraschino

rigaglia (e), giblets

rigata (e), refers to ridges in pasta

rigatoni, large tube-shaped pasta (always has ridges)

rigatoni alla Norma, a Sicilian dish of pasta w/eggplant &
tomato sauce

righini, bluegill

ripieno/ripiene, stuffed

riserva, mature wine

risi e bisi, creamy rice w/green peas.
Bisi is the Venetian word for peas

Risi e Bisi... another favorite. (handwritten)

riso (i), rice

riso ai gamberi, rice w/shrimp

riso alla genovese, rice w/sauce of minced beef (or veal)
w/vegetables

riso alla Greca, rice, vegetables & sausage dish (Greek style)

riso alla milanese, golden rice dish from Milan
featuring saffron

riso alla pilota, rice w/a sausage meat sauce

riso e ceci, broth of rice & chickpeas w/tomatoes & spices

riso in bianco, white rice w/butter

riso in cagnone, boiled rice topped w/*parmesan* cheese

riso mantecado, rice cooked in butter & milk

riso nero, black rice. The rice is made black from squid ink

risoni, rice-shaped pasta for soup

risotto, creamy rice dish w/various ingredients. Served as a
first course, *i primi*, after the *antipasto*

risotto ai fiori di zucca, rice dish made w/a heavy cream base
& zucchini flowers stirred in w/*parmesan*. A Ticino specialty

risotto alla certosina, creamy rice dish w/shrimp, mushrooms,
peas & sometimes frogs' legs

risotto alla mantovana, rice dish w/salami & *parmesan* cheese

risotto alla milanese, rice w/butter, saffron, beef,
zucchini & *parmesan*

risotto alla pescatora, spicy rice w/seafood

risotto alla romana, rice usually w/lamb & potatoes

risotto alla valdostana, rice w/cheese & wine

risotto alla Valenciana, the same dish as Spanish *paella*

risotto alla Veneta, rice w/mussels

risotto alla veronese, rice & ham w/mushrooms

risotto al salto, crisp rice cake

risotto di frutti di mare, rice w/shellfish

risotto di peoci, rice w/mussels

risotto nero, black *risotto.*
Squid or cuttlefish ink makes the rice black

ristretto, reduced broth

robiola, soft, mild & slightly sweet cheese

robiolina, sheep's-milk cheese

rocciate, pastry w/fruit & nuts

rognoncini, kidneys

rognoncini al vino bianco, kidneys in white-wine sauce

rognone (i), kidney

rolatine di vitello, veal cutlets stuffed w/ham &/or cheese

rollè, roll

romagnola, typically, a sauce of tomato, garlic & parsley

romana, alla, a catch-all term that literally means
"Roman style"

rombo, turbot

rosato, rosé

rosbif, roast beef

roscioli, red mullet in Abruzzo

rosé, rosé (blush) wine

rosmarino, rosemary

Rosolio, sweet liqueur

rospo, monkfish/angler fish. *Rospo* also means toad,
so this fish is often referred to as *pesce rospo*

rosso, red

Rosso Antico, cherry-flavored vermouth

rotella, round

rotelle/rotelline, wheel-shaped pasta

rotini, spiral-shaped pasta

rotolo, rolled meat w/stuffing.
Rotolo di spinaci is a spinach roll (pasta w/spinach)

rovi, blackberries

rucola, arugula, also called rocket salad
rughetta, salad green
rujolos, Sardinian sweet-cheese fritters
rum, rum
ruote di carro, pasta in the shape of a wheel (same as *rotelle*)
rustica, alla, usually means a pepper & olive sauce, but can
  mean many things
sagro, sea bream
salame (i), smoked sausage. *Salamino* is a small salami
salame di cioccolato/ salame al cioccolato, chocolate cake in
  the shape of (& looks like) a salami
salamino piccante, pepperoni
salatina, greens for salad
salatini, crackers/snacks
salato, salted/salami
salciccia, sausage
sale, salt
salmi, in, marinated in wine, garlic & herbs (usually w/game)
salmone, salmon. *Salmoncino* is young salmon
salsa, sauce
salsa bianca, white sauce
salsa di pommarola, tomato sauce
salsa di salsiccie, sausage sauce
salsa per la cacciagione, "hunters' sauce" for cooking game
salsa tartara, tartar sauce
salsa verde, parsley-based green sauce (w/oil, lemon juice,
  capers & garlic)
salsicce di maiale, pork sausages
salsiccia (e), fresh sausage
saltato (i)/saltata (e), sautéed
saltimbocca, veal cutlet wrapped
  around ham & sage
salumi, sausages
salumi cotti, cooked sausages & cured meats
salvia, sage
salvietta, napkin (paper)
Sambuca, anise-flavored liqueur. When served *con la mosca*
  ("w/the fly"), the "fly" is a coffee bean in the glass
sanato, young calf
sandwich, sandwich
Sangiovese, dry red wine from Emilia-Romagna
sangue, al, rare

Salame!

Saltimbocca means jump in the mouth.

Sanguinaccio, blood sausage (black pudding).
Also a chocolate spread made from chocolate & pigs' blood

San Pietro, John Dory fish (a firm-textured, white-fleshed fish w/a mild, sweet flavor and low fat content)

San Severo, dry red wine from southern Italy

saor, sweet & sour sauce

sapa, thick sauce made from the juice of freshly pressed grapes

saporito (a), mild/tasty

sarago (saraghi), bluegill

sarda (e)/sardine, sardine

sarda, alla, tomato & meat sauce w/herbs & red wine ("Sardinian style")

sarde a beccaficu, sardines usually stuffed w/pine nuts & raisins. A Sicilian specialty

sardella, fried baby fish minced w/olive oil & powdered peppers from Calabria

sardina, small sardine

sardo, hard, aromatic cheese

sardoncini, little sardines

sartù, baked rice dish w/tomatoes, meatballs & mushrooms

savarin, cake baked in a ring mold & soaked in liquor. The center is filled w/fruit & whipped cream

sbrisolona, flour, cornmeal & almond cake (crumble cake)

scalogno (i), shallot

scaloppa, veal scallop (thin slices of veal)

scaloppa alla fiorentina, veal scallop w/spinach & white sauce

scaloppa milanese, breaded, fried veal scallop

scaloppa napoletana, veal scallop coated in breadcrumbs

scaloppina (e), veal scallop

scaloppine alla boscaiola, veal scallops sautéed in oil & butter & served w/an herb, black olive & onion sauce

scaloppine alla campagnola, veal scallops served in a sauce. The term means "rustic"

scaloppine al marsala, small veal scallops in marsala wine

scaloppine al vino bianco, small veal scallops in white-wine sauce

scamorza, mild cheese (aged *mozzarella*)

scampi, shrimp/prawns

scampi all'Americana, shrimp in a tomato sauce

scanello, sirloin

scapece, fried fish in vinegar & saffron/fried vegetables which are then marinated

scarda, bream (fish)
scarola, escarole (a crispy leaf lettuce)
scarpaccia, zucchini pie (means "old shoe")
scarpena, scorpion fish
scelta, of your choice
schiacciata, flat bread (means "squashed flat")
schila, shrimp in Venice
schmarren, crêpes w/fruit & cream from Trentino-Alto Adige
scialatielli, wide noodles
scialcione, bread loaf
sciroppato (a), cooked in syrup
sciroppo, syrup
sciroppo d'acero, maple syrup
scodella, bowl
scorfano, scorpion fish
scorfano rosso, scorpion fish

scodella.

scorze d'amelle, pasta shaped like slivered almonds found in
    Basilicata
scorzonera, salsify
scotch, scotch
scottadito, grilled lamb chops
scottiglia di cinghiale, wild-boar chops
scrippelle, omelettes cut into thin strips & served in a meat
    broth. A specialty in Abruzzo & Molise
sebadas, bread filled w/cheese & honey, then fried.
    A Sardinian specialty
secco (a), dry. *Funghi secchi* are dried mushrooms
secondo piatto, second course
sedani, the name for a small pasta similar to *rigatoni*
sedano, celery
sedano rapa, celery root
segale, rye
sella, saddle
selvaggina, game/venison
semente/semenza/senze, seeds
semi di, seeds of...
semi di melone, pasta noodle for soup in the shape of
    melon seeds
semifreddi, (half-cold) desserts frozen or refrigerated
    before service
semigreggio integrale, semi-whole wheat rice
semolino, flour

semplice, plain
senape, mustard
senza, without
seppia (e), cuttlefish/squid
seppioline, small cuttlefish/squid
serpentone, pastry stuffed w/chopped figs, apples & nuts
servizio, service/service charge
servizio compreso, service included
servizio incluso, service included
servizio non compreso, service not included
servizio non incluso, service not included
sesamo, sesame
sete, thirsty
sevàdas, Sardinian deep-fried pastries
sfilatino, bread loaf
sfogie, Venetian word for sole
sfoglia/sfogliatella/sfogliatelli, flaky-crusted shell-shaped
    pastry filled w/sweetened *ricotta* cheese
sfogliata, flaky pastry
sfogliata di crema, cream puff
sformato, souffle
sfratti, sweet walnut rolls (a Christmas dessert)
sgavecio, pickled fish
sgombro (i), mackerel
sidro, cider
sigarette, cigarettes
silvano, chocolate tart
Silvestro, herb & mint liqueur
smacafam, *polenta* dish w/*asiago*
    cheese & sausage

Smacafam means hunger killer

Soave, slightly dry white wine from Veneto
sodo/sode, hard boiled
soffritto, sautéed/stock (the base for soup or the sauce for
    pasta) often made w/pigs' organs. Can also refer to slightly
    fried or browned onions, carrots & celery, a base for many
    dishes
sogliola, sole

Sogliola SO-LEE-OH LA

sogliola all'Arlecchino, sole served w/a cream sauce
sogliola alla mugnaia, sole sautéed w/lemon, butter & parsle
sogliola margherita, sole covered w/hollandaise sauce
soia, soy
sopa, soup

sopa cauda, soup w/bread & roast pigeon

soppressa, sausage

soppressata, sausage/sausage made from pig's head

sorbetto, sherbet/sorbet

sorbetto al calvados, sherbet flavored w/apple brandy

sorrentina, often refers to a tomato, basil & mozzarrella sauce

sottaceti, pickles

sottaceto, pickled

sottoaceti, pickled vegetables/pickles

sottofiletto, beef or veal loin

sott'olio, in olive oil

sottonoce, top round of veal

Sotto aceti means under vinegar

spaccatina, bread loaf

spaghetti, spaghetti (long, thin pasta)

spaghetti aglio e olio, spaghetti w/olive oil & garlic

spaghetti alla bolognese, spaghetti w/meat sauce

spaghetti alla carbonara, spaghetti w/cream, bacon,
   cheese & egg

spaghetti alla checca, spaghetti w/raw tomatoes, basil & garlic

spaghetti alla gricia, spaghetti w/onions, bacon, pepper &
   grated cheese

spaghetti all'amatriciana, w/tomato sauce, cheese & garlic

spaghetti alle vongole, spaghetti w/clam sauce

spaghetti al ragù, pasta w/meat & tomato sauce

spaghettini, thin spaghetti

spaghetti pomodoro e basilico, spaghetti w/tomatoes & basil

spalla, shoulder

spanocci, very large prawns

sparaci, asparagus in Venice

sparnocci, type of shrimp

specialità della casa, specialty of the house

specialità di questa regione, specialty of the region

specialità di questo ristorante, specialty of the restaurant

specialità locali, local specialties

specialità regionali, regional specialties/local dishes

speck, cured ham found in the Trentino-Alto Adige region

spelt, a hard wheat

speziato, spicy

spezie, spice

spezzatino, meat or poultry stew/little pieces

spezzato, a stew

spicchio (d'aglio), clove (of garlic)

spiedini alla corsara flambe, grilled meat served "flaming"

spiedini di mare, pieces of grilled fish on a skewer

spiedino (i), any dish roasted on a skewer

spiedo, allo, on a spit

spiga di grano, ear of corn

spigola, sea bass/grouper

spinaci, spinach

spiza di grano, ear of corn

spremuta, fresh fruit drink

spugnola, morel mushroom

spumante, sparkling wine

spumone (i), ice cream w/candied fruit, nuts & whipped cre[...]

spumoni al croccante, *spumoni* topped w/toasted,
    caramelized almonds

spuntatura, breast of...

spuntino, snack

stagionato (a), well aged

stagione (i), season (in season)

starna, a type of partridge

stecca di, bar of

stecchi fritti, fried kebabs

stecchino, toothpick/skewer

Stinco actually means shin bone.

stellette/stelline, star-shaped pasta

stinchetti, marzipan cakes (in the
    shape of human bones)

stinco, braised veal or pork shank. The most common versio[n]
    of this dish is *stinco di maiale al forno*, a whole pork sha[nk]
    oven-roasted w/wine, garlic & rosemary

stoccafisso, dried cod

storione, sturgeon

stracchino, a soft, creamy white cheese

stracciate, scrambled eggs

stracciatella, egg-drop soup. This can also
    refer to chocolate-chip ice cream

stracotto, beef stew w/pork sausage/
    pot roast

strangolapreti, see *strozzapreti*

strangozze, see *stringozzi*

strapazzate, scrambled

strascinati, shell-shaped pasta

stravecchio, *parmesan* cheese aged at least three years

Strega, a strong herb liqueur

strigghie, red mullet in Sicily

stringozzi, a homemade pasta from Umbria

strisce, ribbon noodles

strozzapreti, dumplings or *gnocchi* w/meat sauce.

Strozzapreti means Priest stranglers. A gluttonous priest supposedly choked to death on one.

strudel, this famous pastry roll can be found in Trentino-Alto Adige

strutto, lard

stufatino, pot roast or stew

stufato, braised/stewed/stew

stuzzicadenti, toothpicks

stuzzichino (i), appetizer

succhi di frutta, sweetened fruit juice

succo, juice

succo di frutta, fruit juice

succu tunnu, dumpling soup

Succu tunnu. Never had it but love the name.

sufflé, soufflé

sugna, lard

sugna piccante, a spicy sauce made from pork fat (added to dishes in Basilicata)

sugo, sauce/gravy/juice

sugo, al, w/tomato sauce

suino, pork

suppli/suppli di riso, breaded & deep-fried rice balls usually filled w/ham & cheese

suprema di pollo in gelatina, chicken breast in aspic

suro, mackerel

susina (e), plum

tacchino, turkey

tacchino

TA-KEE.NO

tagliata di manzo, grilled beef

tagliatelle, short ribbon noodles

taglierini, thin noodles

taglierini alla chitarra, a pasta dish featuring a sheet of pasta cut w/a cutter called a *"chitarra"* or guitar

tagliolini, very narrow, thin flat noodles

tajarin, egg noodles found in Piedmont & Valle d'Aosta

taleggio, cheese w/a mild, buttery flavor

taralli, biscuits made in the shape of a ring

tartara, alla, raw w/lemon sauce

tartaruga, turtle

tartina (e), open-faced sandwich/tart.
   Tartine are often appetizers
tartufi di cioccolato, chocolate "truffles"
   (chocolate-coated ice cream)
tartufi di mare, small clams/cockles
tartufo (i), truffle (funghi that grows around tree trunks)
tartufo di gelato, ice cream w/chocolate sauce
tartufo nero, black truffle from Tuscany
tasse, taxes. Menus will often indicate if *tasse e servizio* (taxe
   & service) are included
tavola (o), table
tavola calda, snack bar/fast food
tavoletta di cioccolata, chocolate bar
tazza, cup

TAZZA di té.

tè, tea
tè cinese, Chinese tea
tè d'India, Indian tea
tè freddo, iced tea
tegamaccio, lake-fish stew from Umbria
tegame/tegamino, al, sautéed
teglia, alla, pan-fried
teglia di pesce spada, marinated swordfish dish
tellina (e), clam
teneroni, veal chops
terrina, tureen
testa, head. *Testa di vitello* is calf's head   *I'll pass.*
testina, head
testuggine, turtle
tiedde, fish casserole from Apulia
tiella, any dish with baked layers of ingredients
tiella di agnello, roasted lamb dish
tiella di riso e cozze, mussels, rice & potato dish found in
   Apulia
tigelle, flat bread
timbale/timballo, meat & vegetable casserole w/layers of pa
timo, thyme
tinca (tinche), tench (seafood)
tiramisù, spongecake soaked in
   espresso & brandy w/cream &
   chocolate. *Marsala* can also
   be used in this
   delicious dessert

Tira misu made its way to Italy from the U.S.

tirolese, alla, usually means
   w/fried onion rings
tisana, herbal tea
tisana al cinorrode, rose-hip tea
tisana al tiglio, lime tea
tisana camomilla, camomile tea
tocco di funghi, mushroom sauce
toc de purcit, pork stew w/white wine from
   Friuli-Venezia Giulia
toma, sharp cheese
tomini, fresh cheese from Piedmont
tonarelli/tonarrelli/tonnarelli, thin string pasta
tondino, bread loaf
tonica, tonic water
tonnato, in a tuna sauce. Can also refer to a cold veal dish
tonnetto, small tuna
tonno, tuna
topinambur, artichoke
   (Jerusalem artichoke)
tordo (i), thrush (a bird)
torlo, yolk
torrone, nougat
torta (e), tort/cake/pie

Torrone is immensely popular in Italy.

torta al pesto, spinach & cheese pie/flat
   bread cooked over hot stones in Umbria
   & filled w/cheese, meat or greens
torta di frutta, fruit tart
torta di gelato, ice-cream cake
torta di mele, apple tart
torta di tagliatelle, egg-noodle cake — *yes please.*
torta di verdure, sweet vegetable pie
   (similar to American pumpkin pie)
torta gianduia, chocolate & nut cake
torta meringa, large meringue pie filled w/fruit & topped
   w/whipped cream
torta millefoglie, napoleon (layers of pastry filled w/ice cream
   or whipped cream & topped w/frosting)
torta Pasqualina, Easter puff-pastry cake
torta rustica, cornmeal-cake dessert
torta sbrisolona, flour, cornmeal & almond cake
   (crumble cake)
torta tarantina, potato pie

torta turchesca, rice-pudding tart from Venice

torta zuccotto, liquor-soaked sponge cake filled w/ice
cream or whipped cream, chocolate & candied fruits

tortelli di zucca, pasta stuffed w/pumpkin

tortellini, filled pasta rings

tortello (i), small doughnut/fritter

tortellone (i), a larger *tortellini* pasta

tortiera, cake/pie

tortiglione, almond cakes

tortiglioni, tube-shaped pasta (larger than *cannelloni*)

tortina di marmellata, jam tart

tortini di riso, rice cakes

tortino, tart/cheese & vegetable tart similar to quiche

tortino di carciofi, dish of fried artichokes & eggs

toscana, alla, w/tomatoes & herbs

tostato (a), toasted

totano (i), squid

tournedos, small tenderloin steaks

tovaglia, table cloth

tovagliolo, napkin

Tovagliolo
TOV - A - LEE - OH - LO

tozzetti, hazelnut & almond biscuits (flavored w/anise)

tracina dragone, a fish named "dragon" after its
dangerous spines

tramezzino, small sandwich

trancia/trancio, piece/slice

trattaliu, cooked lamb intestines. A specialty in Sardinia

trenette, long, flat, thin ribbon noodles

trifolati, sliced mushrooms cooked in butter, garlic & oil

trifolato, w/truffles

triglia (e), red mullet

triglia alla Livornese, red mullet cooked w/tomatoes, garlic &
parsley

trigoli, water chestnuts

trippa (e), tripe

trippa alla fiorentina, braised
tripe & minced beef
w/tomato sauce & cheese

trippa alla milanese, tripe
w/onions, carrots, tomatoes,
beans & leeks

trippa alla romana, tripe in a
tomato & vegetable sauce

You can put all the "ALLA's" you want on trippa and it's still TRIPE.

tritato (a), ground (as in ground beef)

trofie, pasta similar to *gnocchi*

trombetta da morto, a type of mushroom

trota (e), trout

trota alle mandorle, stuffed-trout dish

trota di ruscello, river trout

trota iridea, rainbow trout

trota salmonata, salmon trout

trota spaccata, trout split in two, dipped in batter & deep-fried

trotella, trout

tuaca, a mixture of brandy, citrus fruits & herbs

tubetti, *macaroni*

tubi, refers to all tubular pasta

tuorlo, yolk

tutto compreso, all included

ua, grapes in Venice

ubriaco, cooked in red wine

uccelletti/uccelli, small birds (of
    all kinds) usually spit-roasted

uccelletto, all', w/tomato sauce & sage. *Piselli all' uccelleto*
    are peas cooked in tomato sauce w/sage

uccelli scappati, pork, pork sausage &/or small-bird kebabs

ueta, raisin in Venice

uliva, olive

umido, in, stewed

uopa, sea bream

uova, eggs

uova affogate, poached eggs

uova affogate nel vino, eggs poached in wine

uova à la coque, soft-boiled eggs

uova albume, egg whites

uova al burro, eggs fried in butter

uova al guscio, soft-boiled eggs

uova alla campagnola, eggs w/diced vegetables & cheese

uova alla coque, boiled eggs

uova alla fiorentina, fried eggs served on spinach

uova all'americana, fried eggs (usually served w/bacon)

uova alla russa, similar to deviled eggs

uova all'occhio di bue, fried eggs

uova al tegame con formaggio, fried eggs w/cheese

uova barrotte, soft-boiled eggs

uova bollite, soft-boiled eggs

95

uova frittata/uova fritte, fried omelette
uova frittata al pomodoro, tomato omelette
uova frittata al prosciutto, ham omelette
uova in camicia, poached eggs
uova molli/uova mollette, soft-boiled eggs
uova ripiene, stuffed eggs
uova semplice, plain omelette
uova sode agli spinaci, eggs florentine
uova tonnate, hard-boiled eggs in tuna sauce
uovo (a), egg
uovo fritto (uova fritte), fried egg
uovo sodo (uova sode), hard-boiled egg
uovo strapazzatto (uova strapazzate), scrambled egg
uva, grapes
uva bianca, green grapes
uva nera, black grapes
uva passa/uva passita, raisins
uva secca, raisin
uva spina, gooseberry
uvetta, white raisins
vaniglia, vanilla
valdostana, alla, usually means served w/ham & cheese
   (means "Valle d'Aosta style")
valigetta, roasted veal breast
Valpolicella, light (slightly bitter) red wine from Veneto
vapore, a, steamed
vario/vari, assorted
Vecchia Romagna, wine-distilled brandy
vegetable, vegetable
vegetariano (a), vegetarian
velluta, creamy soup
veneziana, alla, w/onions, white wine & sometimes mint
ventaglio, scallop
ventresca, white-meat tuna. Can also mean a boiled pork dish
verde, green/green pasta (w/a spinach base)
verde in pinzimonio, vegetable dip
Verdicchio, a dry white wine from Le Marche
verdura (e), green vegetable
verdura trovata, sautéed wild greens w/potatoes
verdure cotte, cooked vegetables
vermicelli, thin, long spaghetti noodles
vermut, vermouth

verza, cabbage

verzelata, grey mullet

vincigrassi/vincisgrassi, baked lasagna dish. Named after an
   Austrian prince, this dish is a specialty in the region of Le
   Marche where it's usually served w/chicken-giblet sauce

vincotto, a spread made from grapes

vinello, light wine

vino (i), wine

vino amabile, sweet wine

vino asciutto, very dry wine

vino bianco, white wine

vino brut, very dry wine

vino corposo, full-bodied wine

vino da pasto, table wine

vino da tavola, table wine
   (the lowest-quality wine made
   from any combination of grapes)

amabile also means loveable which pretty much refers to all wine as far as we're concerned.

vino del paese, local wine

vino dolce, sweet wine

vino frizzante, sparkling wine

vino leggero, light wine

vino nostrano, local wine

vino novello, new wine

vino rosatello, rosé wine

vino rosato, rosé wine

vino rosé, rosé (blush) wine

vino roseo, rosé wine

vino rosso, red wine

vino da tavola is low quality wine but not necessarily bad.

Vin Santo/Vinsanto, dessert wine from Tuscany & Trentino

vino secco, dry wine

vino semi secco, semi-sweet wine

vino spumante, sparkling wine

vino tipico, local wine

violino, cured leg of goat

visciola, wild cherry

vitellini, very young veal

vitello, veal

vitello all'uccelletto, diced veal & sage simmered in wine

vitello tonnato, cold veal w/tuna sauce

vodka, vodka

vol-au-vents, filled pastry shells

vongola (e), small clam

You weren't really looking this up were you?

vongole, alle, in a clam sauce
vongole oreganate, clams baked or broiled w/oregano
vongole veraci, small clams boiled in vinegar,
  hot pepper & garlic
whisky, whiskey
wurstel, hot dogs (similar to smoked hot dogs)
yogurt/yoghurt, yogurt
yogurt magro, low-calorie yogurt. *Yogurt intero* is not low-fat
zabaglione/zabaione, custard dessert flavored w/Marsala
zafferano, saffron
zalettini, shortbread cookies from Venice *I'll pass.*
zampa (e), pig's (or beef) feet
zampetto, pork leg
zampone, spicy sausage shaped like a pig's foot
zampone di maiale, stuffed pigs' feet
zelten, dried fruit & nut cake from Trentino-Alto Adige
zenzero, ginger
zèppola, doughnut/fritter *– Si, grazie!*
zesti, orange or lemon peel (can also be candied)
ziba, fragrant herb from Sardinia
zimini, in, cooked w/vegetables. *In zimino* can refer to spinach
  or Swiss chard stewed w/cod or squid & tomatoes
zimino, Sardinian fish stew
zingara, alla, "Gypsy style." Each chef has his or her own
  version of this sauce of many ingredients
zite (i), narrow, hollow-tube pasta
zucca, pumpkin or squash
zucca ovifera, squash
zucchero, sugar
zucchero a velo, powdered sugar
zucchero a zollette, lump sugar
zucchero greggio, brown sugar
zucchero grezzo, brown sugar
zucchero in pezzi, lump sugar
zucchero in polvere, powdered sugar *Zuchine* *ZOO·KEEN·E*
zucchine al burro versato, zucchini w/black-butter sauce
zucchine farcite, zucchini filled cheese, ham & mushrooms
zucchine fritte, deep-fried strips of zucchini
zucchine scapecce, pieces of zucchini fried in oil w/garlic
zucchine trifolate, sliced zucchini in butter, parsley & garlic
zucchino (i), zucchini
zucchio, zucchini

zuccotto, ice cream-filled cake
zuchette, zucchini
zuppa, soup
zuppa alla coltivatore, vegetable soup with diced bacon
zuppa alla pavese, soup w/croutons, grated cheese & poached egg
zuppa di arzilla, soup made w/ray fish & broccoli
zuppa di cereali, bean, vegetable & grain stew
zuppa di cipolle alla Francese, french onion soup
zuppa di cozze, mussel soup
zuppa di datteri, fish-soup specialty of Liguria
zuppa di farro, *spelt* (hard wheat) & bean soup
zuppa di frutti di mare, seafood soup
zuppa di pesce, fish stew
zuppa di pollo, chicken soup
zuppa di telline, soup w/tiny clams
zuppa di verdura, vegetable soup
zuppa di vongole, clam soup w/white wine
zuppa d'orzo, barley & potato soup
zuppa fredda, cold soup
zuppa inglese, not a soup at all. Spongecake soaked in liquor
   w/cream filling & whipped cream
zuppa pavese, clear soup w/a poached egg
zuppa valdostana, cabbage soup from the Val d'Aosta region

Zuppa di Farro...
Love it.

Buon Appetito!

Phone numbers, days closed and hours of operation often change, so it's advisable to check ahead. Restaurants in tourist areas may have different hours and days of operation during low season. Reservations are recommended for all restaurants unless noted. The telephone country code for Italy is 39.

Prices are for main courses and without wine. Lunch, even at the most expensive restaurants listed below, always has a lower fixed price. Credit cards are accepted unless noted otherwise.

Inexpensive: under 10 euros
Moderate: 11 – 20 euros
Expensive: 21 – 30 euros
Very Expensive: over 30 euros

We think, hope and pray that our restaurant list is current & correct, but remember... things change. Call first or do a "walk-by" in the afternoon. Stop in, make a reservation — they'll love you for it.

Alberobello
Trullo d'Oro
27 Via F. Cavallotti
Tel. 080/4323909
Closed Sun. (dinner), Mon. and part of Jan.
Unique restaurant in *trulli* (limestone igloo-shaped houses) serving the cuisine of the region of Apulia.
Moderate

Amalfi
La Caravella
12 Via Matteo Camera
Tel. 089/871029
Closed Tues. (in off season) and most of Nov. and Dec.
Family-run restaurant known for seafood dishes, especially *calamari* (squid) and *polpo* (octopus).
Moderate - Expensive

Da Gemma
9 Via Frà Gerardo Sasso
Tel. 089/871345
Closed Wed., and mid-Jan. to mid-Feb.
Specialties of Campania (especially seafood) with summer
dining on the terrace.
Moderate – Expensive

Aosta
Vecchia Aosta
4 Piazza Porta Pretoria
Tel. 0165/361186
Closed Wed., part of Feb. and part of Nov.
Valdostan cuisine (including *fondue*) served in an interesting
maze of dining areas between the inner and outer Roman walls.
Moderate

Ascoli Piceno
Ristorante Tornasacco
36 Piazza del Popolo
Tel. 0736/254151
Closed Fri. and part of July
Taste the specialties of Le Marche at this family-run restaurant.
Inexpensive – Moderate

Assisi
La Fortezza
*2B Vicolo della Fortezza (alley off of the Piazza del
Comune)*
Tel. 075/812418
Closed Thur. and Feb.
Traditional Umbrian dishes (including veal, duck and rab-
bit). Good food at a reasonable price.
Inexpensive – Moderate

Hotel Subasio (Ristorante)
2 Via Frate Elia
075/812206
Umbrian specialties in the shadow of the Basilica of St.
Francis, with the best view in town from the dining terrace. A
great place for a summer lunch.
Moderate

Bergamo
Taverna del Colleoni dell'Angelo
7 Piazza Vecchia
Tel. 035/232596
Closed Mon. and part of Aug.
The specialties of Lombardy and the Lake District served
in a historic building in the heart of the old town.
Moderate – Expensive

Bologna
Anna Maria
17A Via Belle Arti
Tel. 051/266894
Closed Mon., part of Jan. and part of Aug.
Try the homemade pasta in this popular *trattoria* near the
Opera House and the university. The *ragù* is excellent.
Moderate

Da Cesari
8 Via de'Carbonesi (south of Piazza Maggiore)
Tel. 051/237710
Closed Sun., Sat. in July and most of Aug.
Romantic restaurant serving delicious Bolognese dishes
(try the veal Bolognese) along with homemade wine.
Moderate

Osteria Al 15
13 Via Mirasole
Tel. 051/331806
Closed Sun.
Small restaurant with traditional Bolognese dishes. There's
no menu here, the waiters explain the daily offerings. A
great experience.
Moderate

Enoteca Italiana
2B Via Marsala (north of Piazza Maggiore)
Tel. 051/235989
Closed Sun. and most of Aug.
Inexpensive deli and wine bar near the famous Neptune
Fountain.
Inexpensive

Bolzano
Zür Kaiserkron
1 Piazza della Mostra
Tel. 0471/970770
Closed Sat. (dinner) and Sun.
Local dishes of Trentino-Alto Adige, in a historic building
near the Gothic cathedral. The food is Italian with an
Austrian influence.
Moderate – Expensive

Cagliari
Dal Corsaro
28 Viale Regina Margherita
Tel. 070/664318
Closed Sun.
Lively restaurant serving Sardinian specialties such as
porcheddu (roast suckling pig).
Moderate – Expensive

Capri
Da Gemma
6 Via Madre Serafina
Tel. 081/8370461
Closed Mon., Jan. and Feb.
Restaurant-pizzeria serving Caprese specialties (especially
seafood). Try the *fritto alla Gemma* (a mixture of fried
mozzarella, zucchini and vegetables).
Moderate

Le Grottelle
13 Via Arco Naturale
Tel. 081/8375719
Closed Thur.
It's worth the hike for the fabulous views from this rustic
eatery. Try the *ravioli Capri* (ravioli filled with fresh
cheese) and top off your meal with a glass of *limoncello.*
Moderate

Castellina in Chianti
Le Tre Porte
4-6-8 Via Trento e Trieste
Tel. 0577/741163
Closed Tues.
Friendly service at this unassuming restaurant and pizzeria
in a small Tuscan town. Try the *pappardelle sulla lepre*
(strips of pasta w/rabbit sauce).
Moderate

Cernobbio
Il Gatto Nero
69 Via Monte Santa
Tel. 031/512042
Closed Closed Mon. and Tues. (lunch)
This restaurant overlooks Cernobbio and serves the special-
ties of the area surrounding Lake Como (especially fresh
fish). An excellent pine-nut *risotto* is often on the menu.
Moderate

Corniglia
De Mananan
117 Via Fleschi
Tel. 0187/821166
Closed Tues.
Hearty fare served in the cellar of a home in the smallest
Cinque Terre town. Many dishes feature *pesto*. Try the
pansoti (triangular-shaped filled pasta).
Moderate

Florence
Angiolino
36R Via Santo Spirito
Tel. 055/2398976
Closed Mon.
Popular *trattoria* with stone walls, a large wooden stove in
the middle, and wrought-iron fixtures. Good pasta
and meat dishes at reasonable prices.
Inexpensive – Moderate

Buca dell'Orafo
28R Via Volta dei Girolami
Tel. 055/213619
Closed. Sun., Mon., part of Aug. and part of Dec.
No credit cards
Tuscan specialties served in the cellar of a former gold-
smith shop (*orafo*) near the Uffizi.
Moderate

Buca Lapi
1R Via del Trebbio
Tel. 055/213768
Closed Sun. and part of Aug.
This restaurant is in a cellar located under the Palazzo
Antinori. Try the *scampi giganti alla griglia* under the
vaulted ceiling, surrounded by old travel posters.
Moderate – Expensive

Cantinetta Antinori
3 Piazza Antinori
Tel. 055/292234
Closed weekends and Aug.
Tuscan cuisine served in a *palazzo* known for its wine list.
Both a restaurant and wine bar.
Moderate – Expensive

La Carabaccia
190R Via Palazzuolo
Tel. 055/214782
Closed Sun. and Mon. (lunch)
Florentine cuisine at reasonable prices. The specialty here
is *zuppa carabaccia* (creamy onion soup w/croutons).
Moderate

Il Cibrèo
8R Via Verrochio (near Via di San Giuseppe)
Tel. 055/2341100
Closed Sun., Mon. and Aug.
Florentine cuisine at this attractive and popular restaurant,
café and *trattoria*. Try the *sformato* (souffle). The lively
trattoria (Cibreino) does not take reservations.
Moderate (trattoria) – Expensive (restaurant)

Don Chisciotte
4R Via Ridolfi (in the area near Piazza Santa Maria Novella)
Tel. 055/475430
Closed Sun. and Mon. (lunch)
Tuscan restaurant specializing in seafood and known for its
innovative *risotto* dishes.
Expensive

Frescobaldi Wine Bar
2-4R Via dei Magazzini (near Piazza della Signoria)
Tel. 055/284724
Closed Sun. and Mon. (lunch)
Small, attractive wine bar and restaurant with excellent pasta
dishes and a wide selection of wines by the glass.
Inexpensive – Moderate

Mercato Centrale
*Piazzale del Mercato Centrale (off of Via Nazionale near San
Lorenzo)*
Mon. to Sat. 10 a.m. to 2 p.m.
The ground floor of the huge Central Market is loaded with
meat, fish and cheese. Upstairs you'll find fresh produce, wine
and homemade pasta. A great place to stock up for a picnic!

Trattoria Le Mossacce
55R Via del Pronconsolo (near Piazza del Duomo)
Tel. 055/294361
Closed Sat., Sun. and Aug. No reservations
Dine with locals on Florentine cuisine at reasonable prices,
including *ossobuco* (braised veal shank). The restaurant has
been around since the early 1900s.
Inexpensive

Vivoli
7R Via Isola delle Stinche (a backstreet near Santa Croce)
Tel. 055/292334
Closed Mon., Jan. and Aug.
The best ice-cream shop (*gelateria*) in Italy.
Inexpensive

Genoa
Le Cantine Squarciafico
3R Piazza Invrea (near Piazza San Lorenzo)
Tel. 010/2470823
Closed Sun.
You'll sit at long, shared tables in a medieval cellar and dine on *pesto*-based dishes. The specialty here is *stoccafisso* (dried cod).
Moderate

Zeffirino
20 Via XX Settembre
Tel. 010/591990
Open daily. Jacket required
Family-run restaurant since the 1930s. Ligurian specialties such as *frittura del golfa* (mixed fried seafood from the Gulf of Genoa) are served here, and there is a huge wine list.
Expensive

Lerici
Conchiglia
3Piazza del Molo
Tel. 0187/967334
Closed Wed. (except in high tourist season)
Seafront *trattoria* specializing in fresh seafood.
Moderate

Locarno, Switzerland
Ristorante Zurigo
9 Viale Verbano
Tel. 41(country code)/091/7431617
Open daily
Located in a Mediterranean-style hotel, this restaurant serves Italian and Swiss specialties in its dining room and on the lovely terrace. Try the *saltimbocca*!
Moderate – Expensive

Lucca
Giglio
2 Piazza del Giglio
Tel. 0583/494058
Closed Tues. (dinner), Wed., part of Feb. and part of Nov.
A small *trattoria* known for seafood dishes. The homemade
tortellini is delicious.
Moderate

Da Giulio
45 Via delle Conce (Piazza San Donato)
Tel. 0583/55948
Closed Mon. and some Sun.
Locals dine here on Tuscan specialties. Located near the city
walls. No frills here, just hearty food.
Inexpensive – Moderate

Lugano, Switzerland
La Tinera
2 Via dei Gorini
Tel. 41(country code)/091/9235219
Closed Sun. and Aug.
Small cellar *trattoria* serving Ticino specialties in the center of this
historic town. Regional wine is served in traditional ceramic bowls.
Inexpensive – Moderate

Mantua (Mantova)
L'Aquila Nigra
4 Vicolo Bonacolsi
Tel. 0376/327180
Closed most Sun., Mon. and part of Aug.
Elegant dining (featuring the cuisine of Lombardy) in a 15th-
century *palazzo*. Excellent *gnocchi*.
Moderate – Expensive

Matera
Lucanerie
61 Via Santo Stefano
0835/332133
Closed Mon.
Delcious *agnello* (lamb) and other Basilicata dishes.
Moderate

Milan

Bagutta
14 Via Bagutta
Tel. 02/76002767
Closed Sun. and Aug.
Popular *trattoria* serving specialties of Lombardy. There's a huge *antipasto* table. We always have a great time here.
Moderate – Expensive

Biffi
In the Galleria Vittorio Emmanuele
Tel. 02/8057961
A bar and restaurant that's a great place for a snack, lunch or a drink. You can either eat in the restaurant or, for some interesting people-watching, at tables in the *Galleria*.
Moderate

Boeucc
2 Piazza Belgioioso
Tel. 02/76020224
Closed Sat., Sun. (lunch) and Aug.
Milan's oldest restaurant in an elegant setting near the Duomo.
Expensive

Peck
Store: *9 Via Spadari, Tel.02/8023161*
Closed Sun. and Mon. (morning)
Cracco-Peck Ristorante: *4 Via Victor Hugo, Tel. 02/876774*
Closed Sun.
Peck Italian Bar: *3 Via Cesare Cantù, Tel. 02/8693017*
Closed Sun.
A gourmet food store and wine cellar, renowned restaurant and sophisticated wine bar.
Moderate (wine bar) – Expensive (restaurant)

Savini
Galleria Vittorio Emanuele II
Tel. 02/72003433
Closed Sun., part of Jan. and part of Aug.
The best of Lombardy served in the famous and beautiful *Galleria*.
Expensive

Monterosso
Miki
104 Via Fegina (Monterosso al Mare)
Tel. 0187/817608
Closed Tues. from Sep. to July, and all of Nov. and Dec.
Ligurian seafood served in this charming Cinque Terre town.
Enjoy delicious *antipasti* while you take in the sea view.
Moderate

Naples
Brandi
2 Salita Santa Anna di Palazzo (off of Via Chiaia)
Tel. 081/416928
Open daily
Many places claim to have made the first pizza, but it's likely
that the first *pizza margherita* was made here.
Inexpensive – Moderate

Mimì alla Ferrovia
21 Via Alfonso d'Aragona
Tel. 081/5538525
Closed Sun. and part of Aug.
Local favorite for classic Neapolitan cuisine. Try the *linguine
alla Mimì* (flat noodles with a shrimp sauce).
Moderate

La Sacrestia
116 Via Orazio
Tel. 081/664186
Closed Sun. in July and part of Aug.
A view of the harbor and Neopolitan specialties at this
restaurant located in the maze of streets above the port.
Expensive

Orta San Giulio
Olina
40 Via Olina
Tel. 0322/905656
Closed Wed.
Small restaurant/hotel in the center of this picturesque town on
Lake Orta serving the specialties of the Lake District.
Moderate

Orvieto
Le Grotte del Funaro
41 Via Ripa Serancia
Tel. 0763/343276
Closed Mon.
Umbrian specialties served in a *grotte* (cave).
Inexpensive – Moderate

Palermo
Antica Focacceria San Francesco
58 Via Paternostro
Tel. 091/320264
Closed Tues. No credit cards
Stuffed *focaccia* sandwiches and Sicilian snacks at this
1834 bakery in the heart of old town. A great experience!
Inexpensive

Perugia
Il Falchetto
20 Via Bartolo (near Piazza Piccinino)
Tel. 075/5731775
Closed Mon. and part of Jan.
Umbrian specialties in medieval dining rooms. Try the
falchetti (*gnocchi* with ricotta cheese and spinach).
Inexpensive – Moderate

La Taverna
8 Via delle Streghe (off Corso Vannucci)
Tel. 075/5724128
Closed Mon.
Traditional Umbrian food (great lamb) in the heart of the
historic center. Attentive service in a medieval house.
Moderate

Pisa
Da Bruno
12 Via Luigi Bianchi
Tel. 050/560818
Closed Mon. (dinner) and Tues.
Classic Tuscan food near the Leaning Tower. Try the *zuppa
alla paesana* (thick vegetable soup).
Moderate

Portofino
Il Pitosforo
8-9 Via Molo Umberto I
Tel. 0185/269020
Closed Mon., Tues., and Dec. to Feb.
Famous and very expensive, this harborside restaurant serves
Ligurian specialties.
Expensive – Very Expensive

Positano
Buca di Bacco
8 Via Rampa Teglia
Tel. 089/875699
Closed Nov. to Mar.
Specialties of Campania at this seaside restaurant and café. The
speciality here is *zuppa di cozze* (mussel soup).
Expensive

Ravenna
Bella Venezia
16 Via IV Novembre (near the Piazza del Popolo)
Tel. 0544/212746
Closed Sun. and most of Jan.
Family-run restaurant serving homemade pasta and other
specialties of Emilia-Romagna.
Moderate

Rome
Abruzzi
1 Via del Vaccaro (off Piazza Santi Apostoli near Piazza
Venezia)
Tel. 06/6793897
Closed Sat. and part of Aug.
Taste the specialties of the Abruzzo region at this simple *tratto-*
ria. Try the Abruzzi pasta dishes, especially the *cannelloni.*
Inexpensive

Antico Arco
7 Piazzale Aurelio
Tel. 06/5815274
Closed Sun. and part of Aug. No lunch

Attentive service, a modern setting and fine Roman food make this a popular place. Delicious chocolate desserts. It's a little out of the way at the top of Janiculum Hill.
Moderate

Antico Caffè della Pace
3 Via della Pace (near Piazza Navona)
Tel. 06/6861216
Open daily
Attractive cafe with indoor and outdoor seating. Great place for a relaxing drink and snack near the Church of Santa Maria della Pace.
Inexpensive

Arancia Blu
55-65 Via dei Latini (at Via Arunci)
Tel. 06/4454105
No credit cards. No lunch
Inventive vegetarian cuisine (and vegan dishes upon request) at this interesting restaurant in the San Lorenzo area (a neighborhood in transition). Try one of the *ravioli ripieni* (stuffed ravioli) dishes. The good news for vegetarians is that most restaurants offer pasta dishes without meat.
Inexpensive – Moderate

Il Bacaro
27 Via degli Spagnoli
Tel. 06/6864110
Closed Sun.
Small, unpretentious restaurant on a small alley near the Piazza delle Copelle (a huge ivy covers the entrance). Delicious *risotto.*
Moderate

Bistro
40 Via Palestro (near the Termini train station)
Tel. 06/44702868
Closed Sun. (lunch)
Beautiful bistro and wine bar serving interesting dishes such as *taglionini* with lobster (made blue-green with curaçao liqueur). Huge wine list.
Moderate – Expensive

La Campana
18 Vicolo della Campana
Tel. 06/6867820
Closed Mon. and Aug.
Simple Roman fare near the intersection of Via Font.
Borghese and Via della Scrofa near the Piazza Navona. It's
said to be the oldest eatery in Rome. Lots of tourists.
Moderate

La Carbonara
23 Piazza Campo dei Fiori
Tel. 06/6864783
Closed Tues. and part of Aug.
Trattoria serving Roman cuisine including *carbonara*
(hence the restaurant name). On Piazza Campo dei Fiori.
Moderate

Cavour 313
313 Via Cavour (near the Forum)
Tel. 06/6785496
Closed Sun. (June to Sep.), Aug. and no lunch weekends
A huge wine list and selection of cured meats and cheeses
make this a perfect place for a light meal.
Inexpensive

La Cisterna
13 Via della Cisterna
Tel. 06/5812543
Closed Sun.
Regional favorites of the Lazio region served in a family-
run restaurant in Trastevere. Try the grilled *gamberi*
(shrimp).
Moderate

Dal Bolognese
1-2 Piazza del Popolo
Tel. 06/3611426
Closed Mon. and part of Aug.
Bolognese cuisine served on the Piazza del Popolo. Top off
your dinner with a *digestivo* (after-dinner drink) and
dessert at Rosati, the fashionable café next door.
Moderate – Expensive

Enoteca Corsi
89 Via del Gesú (off of Via del Plebescito)
Tel. 06/6790821
Closed Sun. and Aug.
Wine bar serving Roman cuisine at common-seating tables
in a 1937 storefront. An inexpensive choice for lunch.
Inexpensive

'Gusto
9 Piazza Augusto Imperatore (near Via del Corso)
Tel. 06/3226273
Open daily
Something for every food lover! A *pizzeria*, wine bar,
cookware shop and restaurant. Always crowded.
Moderate

I Leoni d'Abruzzo
44 Via Vicenza (near the Termini train station)
Tel. 06/44700272
Closed Sun., Aug. and some winter months
Good food and pleasant service at this (a little too brightly
lit) restaurant. Forget the tourist menu and try the *menu del
giorno* (the menu of the day).
Inexpensive – Moderate

Da Luigi
*24 Piazza Sforza Cesarini (off of Corso Vittorio Emanuele
not too far from Piazza Navona)*
Tel. 06/6865946
Closed Mon.
Outdoor and indoor dining at this *trattoria* on the charming
Piazza Sforza Cesarini. Try the *penne alla vodka*.
Moderate

Nuova Stella
54/58 Via Manin (near Santa Maria Maggiore)
Tel. 06/4875390
Closed Sun.
Family-owned restaurant located near the train station
serving typical Roman fare (including delicious *vitello*
(veal) dishes). Try a bottle of wine from the Lazio region.
Moderate

Orso "80"
33 Via dell'Orso (a short distance north and west of
Piazza Navona)
Tel. 06/6864904
Closed Mon. and Aug.
This restaurant is known for its *antipasto* table as well as
its pasta dishes. Crowded and popular with tourists.
Moderate

Osteria Mia
13 Vicolo della Cancelleria (off of Corso Vittorio
Emanuele not too far from Piazza Navona)
Tel. 06/68892729
Closed Sun.
Friendly *osteria* with a brick-vaulted ceiling and tasty
pasta dishes. The house wine is inexpensive and delicious.
Moderate

Polese
40 Piazza Sforza Cesarini
Tel. 06/6861709
Closed Tues.
Another restaurant on the Piazza Sforza Cesarini. Try the
fettuccine alla Polese (fettuccine w/cream and musrooms).
Inexpensive – Moderate

Porto di Ripetta
250 Via di Ripetta (a few blocks from Piazza del Popolo)
Tel. 06/3612376
Closed Sun.
Dine on Mediterranean cuisine under an attractive brick-
vaulted ceiling.
Moderate

Rosetta
8 Via della Rosetta
Tel. 06/6861002
Closed Sat. (lunch), Sun. (lunch) and part of Aug.
Located near Piazza della Rotonda and the Pantheon, and
known for its seafood. There is no meat on the menu.
Expensive – Very Expensive

Sabatini
13 Piazza Santa Maria in Trastevere (facing the church)
Tel. 06/5812026
Closed part of Aug.
Lively and popular restaurant in Trastevere serving Roman cuisine (especially seafood). Known for its *spaghetti alle vongole* (spaghetti in a white clam sauce).
Moderate – Expensive

La Terrazza
49 Via Ludovisi
Tel. 06/478121
This very expensive and formal restaurant (jacket and tie required) in the Hotel Eden (several blocks off the Via Veneto) offers memorable food and a view of St. Peter's.
Very Expensive

Vecchia Roma
18 Piazza Campitelli
Tel. 06/6864604
Closed Wed. and part of Aug.
A great place to dine outdoors in the summer months, this *trattoria* serves classic Roman fare in the Jewish Ghetto area. Delicious *risotto* dishes.
Moderate

Rome: Food and Wine Stores

Buccone
19 Via di Ripetta (near the Piazza del Popolo)
Tel. 06/3612154
This wine bar is a great place for lunch, and you can also buy wines from every region of Italy.

Castroni
196 Via Cola di Rienzo (near San Pietro)
Tel. 06/6874383
A food market where you can buy specialties from every region of Italy.

Confetteria Moriondo & Gariglio
21-22 Pie di Marmo
Tel. 06/6990856
Small *confetteria* (candy shop). The chocolates are made
on the premises, and the aroma is wonderful.

Enoteca di Sardegna
3 Via della Pigna
Tel. 06/6789374
Tiny shop devoted solely to the wine, liqueurs, cheese,
sweets, pasta and meat from Sardinia.

Ai Monasteri
72 Corso Rinascimento (near Piazza Navona)
Tel. 06/68802783
Wine, liquor, chocolates and other food items produced by
Italian religious orders.

Trimani
20 Via Groito (near Stazione Termini)
Tel. 06/4469661
180-year-old store/bar with over 5,000 wines, liqueurs and
grappas. Over 50 wines by the glass available at the bar.

Rome: Food Markets

Campo dei Fiori (near Piazza Farnese)
6 a.m. – noon, Mon. – Sat.

Piazza Vittorio Emanuele (near Santa Maria Maggiore)
7 a.m. – noon, Mon. – Sat.

San Gimignano
Bel Soggiorno
91 Via San Giovanni
Tel. 0577/940375
Closed Wed., Jan. and Feb.
Tuscan specialties served in a 100-year-old hotel located in
this beautiful walled town. Lots of game dishes on the
menu.
Moderate

Siena
Le Logge
33 Via del Porrione
Tel. 0577/48013
Closed Sun. and part of Jan.
Tuscan dishes at this *osteria* near the Piazza del Campo
(one of Italy's most beautiful squares).
Moderate

Enoteca Italica
Fortezza Medicea/Viale Maccari
Tel. 0577/288497
Closed Sun.
Taste and buy wines from every region of Italy.
Inexpensive

Spoleto
Il Tartufo
24 Piazza Garibadli (near the amphitheater)
Tel. 0743/40236
Closed Sun. (dinner), Mon., part of Jan. and part of July
Spoleto's oldest restaurant has a rustic first floor and
modern second floor. Many dishes (especially the more
expensive ones) feature *tartufi* (truffles).
Moderate

Trieste
Harry's Grill
2 Piazza Unità d'Italia
Tel. 040/7600011
Closed Sun.
This restaurant (located in the Grand Hotel Duchi d'Aosta)
serves international fare, which is appropriate considering
the Italian, Austrian and Slavic influences found here.
Huge wine list.
Moderate – Expensive

Trieste (San Giovanni)
Suban
2 Via Emilio Comici
Tel. 040/54368
Closed Mon. (lunch), Tues. and part of Aug.
In the hills two miles north of Trieste, this *trattoria* serves
specialties of the Friuli-Venezia Giulia region. It's known
for its delicious chicken Kiev.
Moderate

Turin
Al Bicerin
3 Piazza della Consolata
Tel. 011/4369325
Closed Wed.
Founded in 1763, this café is a great place to stop when
visiting the market at nearby Piazza della Repubblica
(Mon. to Sat. 8 a.m.-2 p.m.). You have to order a *bicerin*, a
combination of chocolate, coffee and cream.
Moderate

Da Mauro
21 Via Maria Vittoria
Tel. 011/8170604
Closed Mon. and July
No credit cards. No reservations
Family-run *trattoria* near the Piazza San Carlo serving
Piedmontese and Tuscan dishes. Delicious *cannelloni.*
Inexpensive – Moderate

Porta di Savona
2 Piazza Vittorio Veneto
Tel. 011/8173500
Closed Mon., Tues. (lunch) and part of Aug.
Casual eatery where you'll dine at long wooden tables.
Photos of Old Turin line the walls. Try the *agnolotti* (filled
pasta dishes).
Inexpensive

Vintage 1997
16 Piazza Solferino
Tel. 011/535948
Closed Sat. (lunch), Sun. and part of Aug.
Popular restaurant where you should try the Piedmontese tasting menu when available.
Moderate – Expensive

Venice
Avogaria
1629 Dorsoduro. Calle della Avogaria (near Campo San Sebastiano)
Tel. 041/2960491
San Basilio vaporetto
Closed Tues.
Modern, sleek decor and southern Italian cuisine make this restaurant stand out. You can also sit at the small bar and have appetizers. There's a small courtyard used in warm weather. Fun, friendly and worth the hike.
Moderate

Da Arturo
3656A San Marco. Calle degli Assassini (between Campo San Angelo and Campo Manin off of Calle de la Mandola)
Rialto vaporetto
Tel. 041/5286974
Closed Sun. and Aug.
No credit cards
No seafood at this tiny, popular restaurant. Try the *spaghetti al gorgonzola*.
Moderate – Expensive

La Bitta
2753A Dorsoduro. Calle Lunga San Barnaba (off of Campo San Barnaba)
Ca' Rezzonico vaporetto
Tel. 041/5230531
Closed Sun. No lunch
No credit cards
In a small storefront, this family-owned restaurant focuses on meat dishes (often accompanied by grilled vegetables).
Moderate

Al Covo
3968 Castello. Campiello della Pescaria (off of Riva degli Schiavoni)
Arsenale vaporetto
Tel. 041/5223812
Closed Wed., Thur. and part of Aug.
No credit cards
Fresh Venetian specialties (especially seafood) at this small *osteria*.
Moderate

Enoteca al Volto
4081 San Marco. Calle Cavalli (between the Grand Canal and Salizzada San Luca)
Rialto vaporetto
Tel. 041/5228945
Closed Sun.
No credit cards
This wine bar has wooden tables and chairs, wine labels as wallpaper, an impressive wine list, and simple Venetian fare. A great deal.
Inexpensive

Ai Gondolieri
366 Fondamenta dell'Ospedaleto (near the Guggenheim Museum at Fondamenta Venier dai Leoni)
Accademia vaporetto
Tel. 041/5286396
Closed Tues.
Not for seafood lovers. This restaurant serves meat dishes. Delicious *fiori di zucca* (zucchini flowers filled w/cheese, then battered and fried).
Moderate – Expensive

Da Ivo
1809 San Marco. Calle dei Fuseri (near Campo S. Luca)
San Marco vaporetto
Tel. 041/5285004
Closed Sun. and Jan.
Beautiful restaurant serving Venetian (and Tuscan) specialties. Try the delicious *bistecca alla Fiorentina* (T-bone steak).
Expensive – Very Expensive

Malibran
5864 Cannaregio. Off of Salizzada San Giovanni
Grisostomo and overlooking the Teatro Malibran
Tel. 041/2960768
Open daily
Intimate restaurant, complete with Venetian-glass chande-
liers, near the Rialto Bridge. Italian dishes and homemade
pizza.
Moderate

Al Mascaron
5225 Castello. Calle Lunga Santa Maria Formosa (near
the Campo Santa Maria Formosa)
Rialto vaporetto
Tel. 041/5225995
Closed Sun. and Jan.
No credit cards
You might have to sit next to strangers at long tables in
this unpretentious restaurant/bar. The food is straightfor-
ward Venetian. Try the deep-fried *calamari.*
Moderate

Il Refolo
1459 Santa Croce. Campiello del Piovan (Campo San
Giacomo dell'Orio)
Riva di Biasio or San Stae vaporetto
Tel. 041/5240016
Closed Mon., and Dec. through Mar.
This pizzeria/restaurant is on a picturesque square over-
looking the church of San Giacomo dell'Orio. Customers
dock their boats along the patio for take-out.
Moderate

Da Remigio
3416 Castello. Salizzada dei Greci
Riva del Schiavoni vaporetto
Tel. 041/5230089
Closed Mon. (dinner), Tues., part of July and part of Aug.
Small, family-style Venetian *trattoria* serving seafood
(usually grilled and sold by weight), pasta and meat dishes.
Inexpensive – Moderate

Taverna la Fenice
1939 San Marco. Campiello de la Fenice (near La Fenice
Opera House off of Calle de la Fenice)
San Marco vaporetto
Tel. 041/5223856
Closed Mon.
Elegant Venetian and Italian dining (indoors and outdoors).
Try the *tagliatelle* with cream sauce.
Moderate – Expensive

Trattoria alla Madonna
592-594 San Polo. Calle della Madonna
Rialto vaporetto
Tel. 041/5223824
Closed Wed., Jan. and part of Aug.
Near the Rialto, this *trattoria* specializes in fresh grilled fish.
You will also find pasta and meat dishes, and Venetian spe-
cialties such as *fegato alla veneziana* (liver and onions).
Moderate

Vini da Gigio
3628A Cannaregio. Fondamenta San Felice (just off the
Strada Nuova)
Cá d'Oro vaporetto
Tel. 041/5285140
Closed Mon., Tues., part of Jan. and part of Aug.
Wine bar and *osteria* serving Venetian specialties and home-
made pasta. Delicious *gnocchi.*
Moderate – Expensive

Vino Vino
2007A San Marco. Ponte delle Veste (between La Fenice and
via XXII Marzo)
S. Maria del Giglio vaporetto
Tel. 041/2417688
Closed Tues.
Popular wine bar and restaurant serving typical Venetian cui-
sine and offering 350 Italian and imported wines by the bottle
or glass.
Inexpensive

Venice: Food Markets

Rialto Bridge (Rialto vaporetto)
7 a.m. – 1 p.m., Mon. – Sat.

Via Garibaldi (Arsenale vaporetto)
mornings., Mon. – Fri.

Venice: *Cicheti* Bars

Here are a few places to try *cicheti*, the Venice version of *tapas*. (*Rialto vaporetto*).

Osteria alla Botte
5482 Calle della Bissa (east end of the Rialto Bridge near Campo San Bartolomeo)
Tel. 041/5209775
Closed Thur. and Sun.

Osteria Sora al Ponte
1588 Ponte delle Beccarie (near the Rialto Bridge Market off of Campo de la Beccarie)
Tel. 041/718208
Closed Mon.

Bancogiro
122 Campo San Giacometto (west end of Rialto Bridge along the Grand Canal)
Tel. 041/5232061
Closed Sun. (dinner) and Mon.

Vernazza
Gambero Rosso
7 Piazza Marconi
Tel. 0187/812265
Closed Mon., Jan. and Feb.
Ligurian specialties at this Cinque Terre restaurant (it's been open for over 100 years) located on the harbor. The creamy *pesto* is fantastic.
Moderate

Restaurants by Location

Descriptions of restaurants in the cities listed here can be found on the page number following each city.

RESTAURANT AND FOOD NOTES

Your Menu Translators and Restaurant Guides!

Eating & Drinking in Paris
Eating & Drinking in Italy
Eating & Drinking in Spain
Eating & Drinking in Latin America

Written by
Andy Herbach and Michael Dillon

Published by
Open Road Publishing

Distributed by
Simon & Schuster